This book belongs to:

_____

Cancer Daily Horoscope 2023

Copyright © 2022 by Crystal Sky
www.Mystic-Cat.com

All rights reserved. This book or any portion thereof may not be copied or used in any manner whatsoever without the publisher's express written permission except for the use of brief quotations in a book review.

The information accessible from this book is for informational purposes only. No statement within is a promise of benefits. There is no guarantee of any results.

Images are under license from Shutterstock, Dreamstime, Canva, or Depositphotos.

Cancer Daily Horoscope 2023

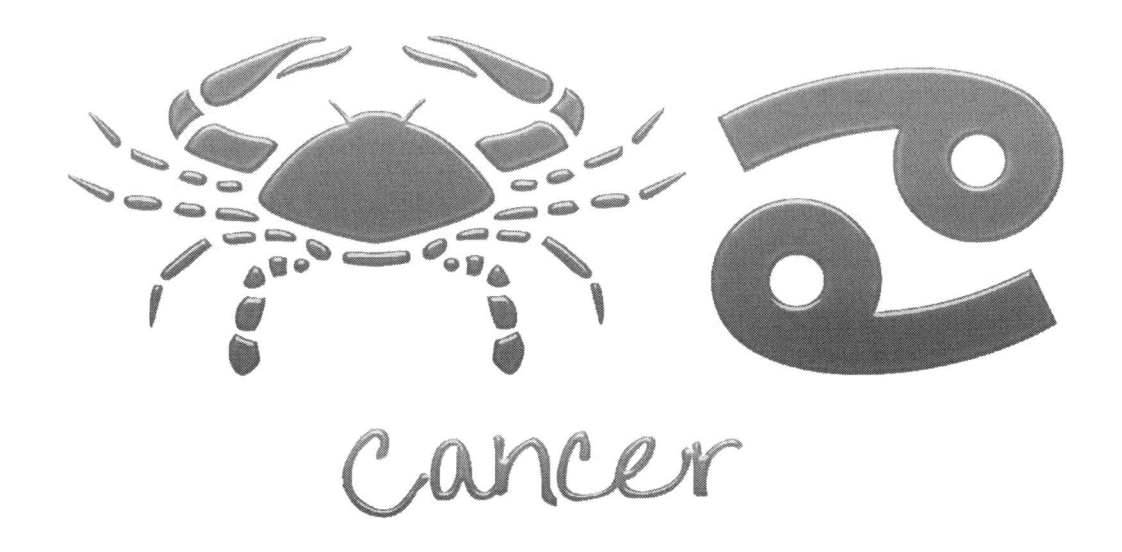

2023

JANUARY	FEBRUARY	MARCH	APRIL
M T W T F S S	M T W T F S S	M T W T F S S	M T W T F S S
1	1 2 3 4 5	1 2 3 4 5	1 2
2 3 4 5 6 7 8	6 7 8 9 10 11 12	6 7 8 9 10 11 12	3 4 5 6 7 8 9
9 10 11 12 13 14 15	13 14 15 16 17 18 19	13 14 15 16 17 18 19	10 11 12 13 14 15 16
16 17 18 19 20 21 22	20 21 22 23 24 25 26	20 21 22 23 24 25 26	17 18 19 20 21 22 23
23 24 25 26 27 28 29	27 28	27 28 29 30 31	24 25 26 27 28 29 30
30 31			

MAY	JUNE	JULY	AUGUST
M T W T F S S	M T W T F S S	M T W T F S S	M T W T F S S
1 2 3 4 5 6 7	1 2 3 4	1 2	1 2 3 4 5 6
8 9 10 11 12 13 14	5 6 7 8 9 10 11	3 4 5 6 7 8 9	7 8 9 10 11 12 13
15 16 17 18 19 20 21	12 13 14 15 16 17 18	10 11 12 13 14 15 16	14 15 16 17 18 19 20
22 23 24 25 26 27 28	19 20 21 22 23 24 25	17 18 19 20 21 22 23	21 22 23 24 25 26 27
29 30 31	26 27 28 29 30	24 25 26 27 28 29 30	28 29 30 31
		31	

SEPTEMBER	OCTOBER	NOVEMBER	DECEMBER
M T W T F S S	M T W T F S S	M T W T F S S	M T W T F S S
1 2 3	1	1 2 3 4 5	1 2 3
4 5 6 7 8 9 10	2 3 4 5 6 7 8	6 7 8 9 10 11 12	4 5 6 7 8 9 10
11 12 13 14 15 16 17	9 10 11 12 13 14 15	13 14 15 16 17 18 19	11 12 13 14 15 16 17
18 19 20 21 22 23 24	16 17 18 19 20 21 22	20 21 22 23 24 25 26	18 19 20 21 22 23 24
25 26 27 28 29 30	23 24 25 26 27 28 29	27 28 29 30	25 26 27 28 29 30 31
	30 31		

2023 AT A GLANCE

Eclipses

Hybrid Solar – April 20th

Penumbral Lunar – May 5th

Annular Solar – October 14th

Partial Lunar - October 28th

Equinoxes and Solstices

Spring - March 20th 21:25

Summer - June 21st 14:52

Fall – September 23rd 06:50

Winter – December 22nd 03:28

Mercury Retrogrades

December 29th, 2022 Capricorn - January 18th Capricorn

April 21st Taurus – May 15th Taurus

August 23rd Virgo – September 15th Virgo

December 13th Capricorn - January 2nd, 2024 Sagittarius

2023 FULL MOONS

Wolf Moon: January 6th, 23:09

Snow Moon: February 5th, 18:30

Worm Moon March 7th, 12:40

Pink Moon: April 6th, 4:37

Flower Moon: May 5th, 17:34

Strawberry Moon: June 4th, 3:42

Buck Moon: July 3rd, 11:40

Sturgeon Moon: August 1st, 18:32

Blue Moon: August 31st, 1:36

Corn, Harvest Moon: September 29th, 9:58

Hunters Moon: October 28th, 20:23

Beaver Moon: November 27th, 9:16

Cold Moon: December 27th, 0:34

2023 INGRESSES

Mars Ingresses

Mar 25, 2023, 11:36	Mars enters Cancer
May 20, 2023, 15:24	Mars enters Leo
Jul 10, 2023, 11:34	Mars enters Virgo
Aug 27, 2023, 13:15	Mars enters Libra
Oct 12, 2023, 3:39	Mars enters Scorpio
Nov 24, 2023, 10:10	Mars enters Sagittarius

Venus Ingresses

Jan 3, 2023, 2:06	Venus enters Aquarius
Jan 27, 2023, 2:29	Venus enters Pisces
Feb 20, 2023, 7:52	Venus enters Aries
Mar 16, 2023, 22:31	Venus enters Taurus
Apr 11, 2023, 4:43	Venus enters Gemini
May 7, 2023, 14:20	Venus enters Cancer
Jun 5, 2023, 13:42	Venus enters Leo
Oct 9, 2023, 1:06	Venus enters Virgo
Nov 8, 2023, 9:27	Venus enters Libra
Dec 4, 2023, 18:48	Venus enters Scorpio
Dec 29, 2023, 20:21	Venus enters Sagittarius

Mercury Ingresses

Feb 11, 2023, 11:22	Mercury enters Aquarius
Mar 2, 2023, 22:49	Mercury enters Pisces
Mar 19, 2023, 04:22	Mercury enters Aries
Apr 3, 2023, 16:20	Mercury enters Taurus
Jun 11, 2023, 10:24	Mercury enters Gemini
Jun 27, 2023, 0:22	Mercury enters Cancer
Jul 11, 2023, 4:09	Mercury enters Leo
Jul 28, 2023, 21:29	Mercury enters Virgo
Oct 5, 2023, 0:06	Mercury enters Libra
Oct 22, 2023, 6:46	Mercury enters Scorpio
Nov 10, 2023, 6:22	Mercury enters Sagittarius
Dec 1, 2023, 14:29	Mercury enters Capricorn

Slower Moving Ingresses

Mar 7, 2023, 13:03	Saturn enters Pisces
Mar 23, 2023, 8:42	Pluto enters Aquarius
May 16, 2023, 17:01	Jupiter enters Taurus

The Moon Phases

- New Moon (Dark Moon)
- Waxing Crescent Moon
- First Quarter Moon
- Waxing Gibbous Moon
- Full Moon
- Waning Gibbous (Disseminating) Moon
- Third (Last/Reconciling) Quarter Moon
- Waning Crescent (Balsamic) Moon

⏺ New Moon (Dark Moon)

The New Moon reveals what hides beyond the realm of everyday circumstances. It creates space to focus on contemplation and the gathering of wisdom. It is the beginning of the moon cycles. It is a time for plotting your course and planning for the future. It does let you unearth new possibilities when you tap into the wisdom of what is flying under the radar. You can embrace positivity, change, and adaptability. Harness the New Moon's power to set the stage for developing your trailblazing ideas. It is a Moon phase for hatching plans for nurturing ideas. Creativity is quickening; thoughts are flexible and innovative. Epiphanies are prevalent during this time.

⏺ Waxing Crescent Moon

It is the Moon's first step forward on her journey towards fullness. Change is in the air, it can feel challenging to see the path ahead, yet something is tempting you forward. Excitement and inspiration are in the air. It epitomizes a willingness to be open to change and grow your world. This Moon often brings surprises, good news, seed money, and secret information. This Moon brings opportunities that are a catalyst for change. It tempts the debut of wild ideas and goals. It catapults you towards growth and often brings a breakthrough that sweeps in and demands your attention. Changes in the air inspiration weave the threads of manifestation around your awareness.

◐ First Quarter Moon

The First Quarter Moon is when exactly half of the Moon is shining. It signifies that action is ready to be taken. You face a crossroads; decisive action clears the path. You cut through indecisiveness and make your way forward. There is a sense of something growing during this phase. Your creativity nourishes the seeds you planted. As you reflect on this journey, you draw equilibrium and balance the First Quarter Moon's energy before tipping the scales in your favor. You feel a sense of accomplishment of having made progress on your journey, yet, there is still a long way to go. Pause, contemplate the path ahead, and nurture your sense of perseverance and grit as things have a ways to go.

◐ Waxing Gibbous Moon

Your plans are growing; the devil is in the detail; a meticulous approach lets you achieve the highest result. You may find a boost arrives and gives a shot of can-do energy. It connects you with new information about the path ahead. The Moon is growing, as is your creativity, inspiration, and focus. It is also a time of essential adjustments, streamlining, evaluating goals, and plotting your course towards the final destination. Success is within reach; a final push will get you through. The wind is beneath your wings, a conclusion within reach, and you have the tools at your disposal to achieve your vision.

Full Moon

The Full Moon is when you often reach a successful conclusion. It does bring a bounty that adds to your harvest. Something unexpected often unfolds that transforms your experience. It catches you by surprise, a breath of fresh air; it is a magical time that lets you appreciate what your work has achieved. It is time for communication and sharing thoughts and ideas. It often brings a revelation eliminating new information. The path clears, and you release doubt, anxiety, and tension. It is a therapeutic and healing time that lets you release old energy positively and supportively.

Waning Gibbous (Disseminating) Moon

The Waning gibbous Moon is perfect for release; it allows you to cut away from areas that hold back true potential. You may feel drained as you have worked hard, journeyed long, and are now creating space to return and complete the cycle. It does see tools arrive to support and nourish your spirit. Creating space to channel your energy effectively and cutting away outworn regions creates an environment that lets your ideas and efforts bloom. It is a healing time, a time of acceptance that things move forward towards completing a cycle. This the casting off the outworn, the debris that accumulates over the lunar month is a vital cleansing that clears space and resolves complex emotions that may cling to your energy if not addressed.

🌗 Third (Last/Reconciling) Quarter Moon

This Moon is about stabilizing your foundations. There is uncertainty shifting sands; as change surrounds your life, take time to be mindful of drawing balance into your world. It is the perfect time to reconnect with simple past times and hobbies. Securing and tethering your energy does build a stable foundation from which to grow your world. It is time to take stock and balance areas of your life. Consolidating your power by nurturing your inner child lets you embrace a chapter to focus on the areas that bring you joy. It is not time to advance or acquire new goals. It's a restful phase that speaks of simple pastimes that nurture your spirit.

🌘 Waning Crescent (Balsamic) Moon

The Waning Crescent Moon completes the cycle; this Moon finishes the set. It lets you tie up loose ends, finish the finer details, and create space for new inspiration to flow into your world once the cycle begins again. The word balsamic speaks of healing and attending to areas that feel raw or sensitive. It is a mystical phase that reconnects you to the cycle of life. As the Moon dies away, you can move away from areas that feel best left behind. Focusing on healing, meditation, self-care, and nurturing one's spirit is essential during this Moon phase.

🌑 The Full Moon: How it can affect your star sign

The Full Moon shines a light on areas that seek adjustment or healing in your life.

The Full Moon is a time to bring awareness into your spirit of the areas that seek resolution or adjustment. Over time, the past can create emotional blockages in your life. The Full Moon forms a sacred space to process sensitive emotions and release the past's hold on your spirit.

This lunar vibration brings awareness to your spirit of how your emotions affect your daily life. When the Moon is complete, your emotional awareness magnifies, and you feel things more intensely in your everyday life.

The Full Moon brings a chance to go over inner terrain and connect with your intuition. She shines a light on areas that hold the most significant meaning in your life. This effect has a powerful impact on creativity, planning, and future life direction. Listening to your gut instincts helps you strip away from areas that only cloud judgment and muddy your awareness.

Cancer: Be mindful of emotions that rise to the surface. The healing aspect can trigger sensitivities that feel like a tsunami washing over your spirit. Take time to unpack each memory and gently release sensitive areas. Pay close attention to what surfaces under the Full Moon. Expect sharp insights and hidden information to appear. Resolving sensitive emotions promotes stability that gets you back on track after your Full Moon healing finishes.

I use the 24-hour clock/military time.
Time set to Coordinated Universal Time Zone (UT±0)

I've noted Meteor Showers on the date they peak.

January

Sun	Mon	Tue	Wed	Thu	Fri	Sat
1	2	3	4	5	6	7
8	9	10	11	12	13	14
15	16	17	18	19	20	21
22	23	24	25	26	27	28
29	30	31				

NEW MOON

Wolf Moon

December/January

30 Friday

Focusing on the basics takes you towards improving the foundations in your life. As you peel back the layers, you reveal refreshing potential which revolutionizes your life. It lets you proactively nurture your environment and harness the power of manifestation to achieve a pleasing result. It underscores an atmosphere of personal growth that puts you on a path towards growing your life. You reveal a journey ripe with potential ready to blossom.

31 Saturday

Things are on the move for your life soon. An area you nurture brings an active time of growth and expansion. It lets you touch down on developing your goals with abandon. A freedom-driven chapter lights up pathways that allow you to promote your rebellious tendencies. It lets you set sail on a voyage that offers happiness and connection. It connects you with kindred spirits who bring a celebration into your life.

1 Sunday ~ New Year's Day, Venus conjunct Pluto 5:24

Venus, the ruler of love, offers an abundant landscape when conjunct with Pluto. The energy of transformation surrounds your life, enabling you to advance your romantic life. It fuels your spirit with the news that helps you create a bridge towards a brighter future. A refreshing change arrives around your personal life; it brings meaningful conversations that let you map goals.

January

2 Monday ~ Mercury sextile Neptune 6:53

This sextile attracts free-flowing and creative ideas that help you place the cherry on top of this year's plans and aspirations. It amplifies potential and offers a path that captures the essence of inspiration. Igniting the fires of your creativity adds fuel and motivation to get the ball rolling on developing a new area. It brings a landscape of refreshing options which weaves magic into your life.

3 Tuesday ~ Venus ingress Aquarius 2:06, Quadrantids Meteors runs Jan 1st – 5th

Focused and determined, you unearth new leads that take your abilities forward. It brings a time of building a secure foundation and progressing towards growing your career path. It gets an upgrade that may feel subtle at first but soon opens pathways towards growth. It brings balance and stability, and this becomes the basis from which you advance your abilities forward.

4 Wednesday ~ Venus sextile Jupiter 9:07

This sextile attracts warm and abundant energy into your social life. A dash of luck and good fortune combined with enriching conversations improve social bonds in your life. It offers a remarkable shift forward that takes you toward a happier chapter. Your life benefits from lightness and harmony when news arrives that releases worries and begins a new chapter of inspiration. Signs ahead shape up a prosperous path of improving your world.

5 Thursday ~ Sun trine Uranus 16:43

This Sun trine Uranus transit brings positive change and excitement flowing into your world. It brings options and opportunities to propel you forward toward new adventures. It brings a time of generating leads and mapping out a strategy for future development. It brings growth and stability that opens the path forward. As you discover a role that beautifully blends your skills, a curious area calls your name.

January

6 Friday ~ Wolf Full Moon in Cancer 23:09

You head towards an extended time that reinvents the potential possible. It speaks of a transformational aspect that has a profound effect on improving the circumstances in your world. You discover a path that offers exciting potential; it grows your world outwardly. It centers around developing unique goals that nurture harmony and well-being in your life.

7 Saturday ~ Sun Conjunct Mercury 12:56

This conjunct bodes well for communication. Rising prospects draw insightful conversations that stimulate creativity and problem-solving mental energy. You are on the cusp of a new journey forward that lets you take advantage of a growth aspect that offers lucrative benefits. Strategizing and brainstorming in a group environment draws a pleasing result. It paves the way forward for developing an enterprising area of interest.

8 Sunday ~ Mercury trine Uranus 23:22

Mercury forming a trine with Uranus brings flashes of insight; expect an epiphany as brilliance surrounds your thought processes today. You come up with new options to improve the time spent at home. It brings a fruitful time that provides you with an outlet for your creative energy. It brings an enjoyable chapter that grows your foundation, drawing stability and balance into your life. You can reap great rewards by nurturing your creativity.

January

9 Monday ~ Venus trine Mars 15:21

This week, Venus trine Mars raises your energy and brings a vibrant passion for life. You may be feeling restless; a journey of new horizons is looming overhead. It sparks movement and discovery in your life. It lets you take a break into something meaningful that makes you a priority. It does place a focus on nurturing your life. Your hunger for knowledge becomes a quest to explore new goals as your vision for future growth takes shape.

10 Tuesday

An area you become involved with developing takes on great importance in your life. It brings an active time of progressing your dreams, creating a positive shift forward that releases the pressure. It stabilizes foundations and brings a much-needed downtime. Moving past the barriers, you discover a landscape ripe with possibility. It gets more outstanding balance and stability into your world that offers an essential upgrade.

11 Wednesday

Life opens to a unique flavor that has you feeling optimistic. An opportunity comes knocking, creating space to develop a dream project. Focusing on developing your skills cultivates an enterprising time that tempts you forward. You unearth a journey of advancement that takes your abilities to the next level. It lights a passage towards improving the potential in your world. Rising prospects break up stagnant patterns and head you towards a refreshing change.

12 Thursday ~ Mars turns direct at 20:54

With the planet Mars moving forward, your energy, passion, and drive return full force. It brings forward momentum that lifts the lid on releasing restrictions that currently hold you back. It offers a fresh start that draws stability into your career path. It brings an innovative and abundant landscape that nurtures creativity. Clearing away limitations lets you move forward with purpose. It brings significant change, which marks expansion.

January

13 Friday ~ Sun sextile Neptune 14:11

Resources and support help you get busy manifesting your vision. Goodness and joy flow into your world. It does help you appreciate the blessings that surround your life. You soon arrive at a chapter that resonates with tranquility and contentment. A vital reward lets you expand your horizons and make headway towards your vision. Setting aside fears, you can trust that things are heading in the right direction.

14 Saturday

Capturing the essence of an abundant mindset offers a new approach that draws well-being into your life. Being open to change draws a pleasing result for your social life. Weeding out areas that limit progress helps you achieve a beautiful shift forward. It brings headway around developing life. This progression lets you dive into a refreshing aspect that ignites the more significant potential in your world. A slow and steady approach offers a landscape of possibility

15 Sunday ~ Venus square Uranus 1:21, Last Quarter Moon in Libra 2:12

A Venus Uranus square creates a need to balance and harmonize interpersonal bonds while honoring your need for freedom and expression. Setting appropriate boundaries limits the drama; it helps release outworn energy. It brings a focus on developing your world as you get busy working with a path that offers room for progression. It brings pep into your life as a burst of new energy makes a striking mark on your world.

January

16 Monday ~ Martin Luther King Day

A more stable landscape will emerge soon. It does bring a welcome shift forward that increases the potential possible. Life expands at a comfortable pace as you draw profitable opportunities to improve your circumstances. It does let you embrace life-affirming endeavors that stabilize and bring balance into your environment. Friends tempt you out into the broader community.

17 Tuesday

Crafting your vision for future growth promotes an environment that nurtures your talents. You advance life forward and develop your skills in a new area. You are on a continuous cycle of evolution, growth, and change. Broadening your horizons offers an uplifting trajectory that connects with unique opportunities. Fine-tuning your talents enables you to achieve mastery in your chosen field.

18 Wednesday ~ Mercury turns direct at 13:12

Mercury is the messenger planet of communication, collaboration, and creative expression. Life becomes more manageable and flows more easily during Mercury's direct phase. A new cycle of life awaits discovery. Breaking free from limitations and expanding your life brings unique adventures that reveal a journey that blossoms into a meaningful path forward.

19 Thursday

You benefit from events on the horizon as it gives you the green light to develop dreams and growth journeys. Opportunity comes knocking, which provides an exciting sign that things are turning in your favor. Life is ripe with potential ready to blossom. Navigating the ever-changing environment brings agility and adaptability, laying the groundwork for a stable basis for growing your life.

January

20 Friday ~ Sun ingress Aquarius 8:26

Directing your energy towards areas with the most significant meaning helps you thrive and prosper. It highlights a social aspect that brings people together in an engaging group environment. Improving social bonds cracks the code to a brighter chapter. It brings a shift towards expansion that extends the borders of your life. A social aspect ahead gets a sweet surprise that shines a spotlight on improving the potential in your world.

21 Saturday ~ New Moon in Aquarius 20:54

News arrives that brings excitement into your life. It has you feeling optimistic about rising prospects that bring new options. It leads to a time that pushes back boundaries and overcomes the limitations as you dive deep into developing your vision. A unique landscape tempts you forward as your imagination ignites with fresh inspiration. Priorities and plans soon take shape. It elevates your abilities and opens a pathway toward growth and prosperity.

22 Sunday ~ Venus conjunct Saturn 22:12, Uranus turns direct 23:23
Chinese New Year (Rabbit)

The Chinese New Year heralds good luck and fortune. Rabbits are a symbol of growth and fertility. Ideas planted in fertile terrain will get a chance to blossom and grow. Blending these elements lets you craft a path that aligns with your vision for future growth. An opportunity comes knocking that offers a chance to spread your wings in a new area.

January

23 Monday

Exploring leads and researching options helps you come up with a winning trajectory. It provides you with an approach that lets you chase your vision for future growth. You soon build stable foundations that heighten the security in your life. Climbing the rungs ahead sees you reaching for success. It does allow things to move forward quickly as you draw a stable foundation from which to grow your vision.

24 Tuesday

A high degree of self-sufficiency draws a grounded and peaceful working environment. It lets you take on an enterprising area that offers rising prospects. New possibilities arrive to keep your focus on expanding life forward towards greener pastures. Life becomes a blur of refreshing options that keep you motivated and optimistic about prospects.

25 Wednesday ~ Sun sextile Jupiter 1:30

In sextile with Jupiter, the Sun attracts a restless vibe that has you yearning to expand your life outwardly. Good fortune lights a shimmering path forward that makes you eager to embark on a new journey. Upcoming potential increases good fortune, leading to an uptick of options that grow your world. It brings a potent time for change and evolution. Your talents and experience crack the code to a prosperous chapter.

26 Thursday

Improving the basis of your foundations brings structure and balance. It reawakens creativity and brings growth to the forefront of your life. You optimize your circumstances by exploring various avenues of possibility. Investigating unique options brings a steady growth cycle that has you working smarter, not harder. You use creativity to develop innovative solutions that offer new flavors to your life.

JANUARY

27 Friday ~ Venus ingress Pisces 2:29

News arrives out of the blue that opens your life up to a positive trend. It connects you with someone who offers engaging advice and seeks to promote expansion in your life. It brings an invitation to mingle that leads to soul-stirring discussions and happy trails forward for your social life. A lively exchange emphasizes improvement and this sense of connection leaves you feeling optimistic about future potential.

28 Saturday ~ First Quarter Moon in Taurus 15:19

Expansion around your social life guides the path ahead. A flow of manifestation brings sunny skies overhead. It paves the way towards progressing a bond that nurtures abundance and well-being in your life. Lively discussions and in-depth communication deliver exciting possibilities. It translates to a time that builds your confidence and renews your spirit. It shines a light on a journey that glimmers with gold.

29 Sunday

A flood of communication draws an invite that cracks the code to expand your social life. It offers a time of transformation that grows your world on many levels. It brings an opportunity to share communication with someone you value. Improving the foundations in your life draws happiness and harmony. Enthusiasm rises as you head towards an upswing of possibility that begins a new cycle.

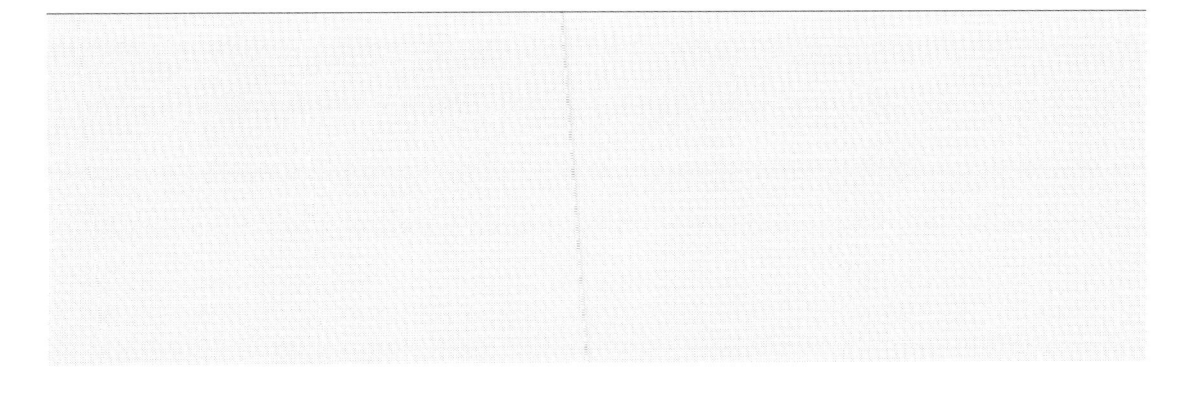

February

Sun	Mon	Tue	Wed	Thu	Fri	Sat
			1	2	3	4
5	6	7	8	9	10	11
12	13	14	15	16	17	18
19	20	21	22	23	24	25
26	27	28				

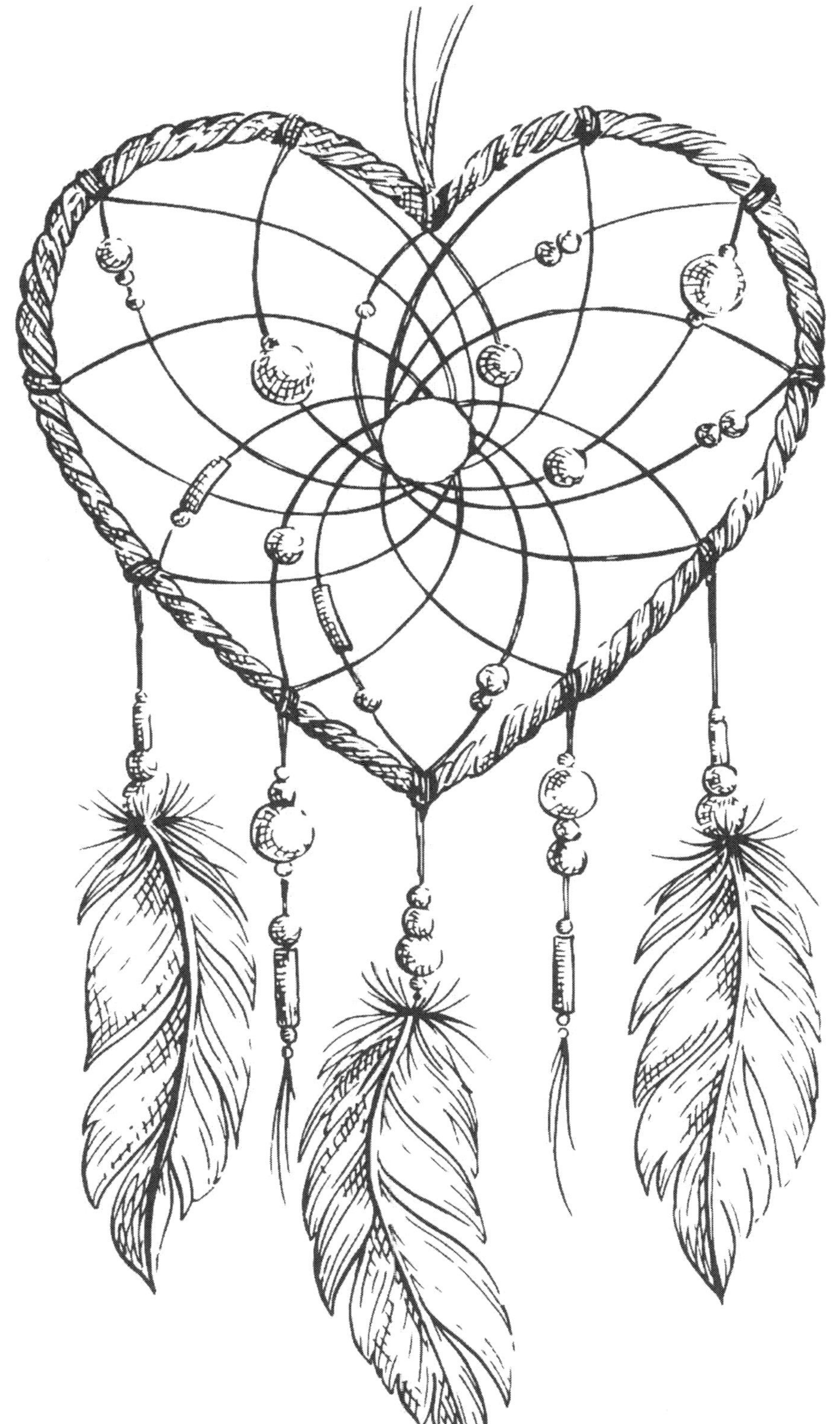

New Moon

Snow Moon

January/February

30 Monday ~ Sun trine Mars 1:45, Mercury trine Uranus 2:17
Mercury at Greatest Eastern Elongation: 25.0°W

A new chapter opens in your life when news arrives out of the blue. It brings a faster-moving pace that takes you towards developing working goals. You attract abundance, supporting and sustaining you as you expand your talents into new areas. It brings a beautiful picture of what is possible when you take action and grow your dreams. It offers room to develop your abilities.

31 Tuesday

Rising prospects ahead help you make the most of new opportunities that tempt you forward. Taking time to plan for future contingencies enables you to pivot away from issues and connect with growing the path ahead, exploring new pathways of light on the way forward. More positive energy is ready to emerge in your life. This lighter vibe sets you out on an adventure that offers an exciting journey ahead.

1 Wednesday ~ Imbolc

Action and thought in motion weave beautiful energy into your life. It brings a prime time to contemplate future goals and focus your resources on establishing areas that catch your interest. There is much to look forward to ahead as an opportunity crosses your path that marks the start of a refreshing chapter of growth and rising prospects in your life.

2 Thursday~ Groundhog Day

Well-crafted ideas soon get a chance to be shared with kindred folk. It draws light-hearted discussions that blaze a trail towards developing new goals in your life. As you focus on the journey ahead, you discover that life rewards you. News is incoming, which offers a pleasing result as it shines a light on an area worth your time.

FEBRUARY

3 Friday

You enter a time of rising prospects that brings news your way. Lovely changes become a gateway from which to grow your social life. It gets the ball rolling on building stable foundations and connecting with friends and companions. A whirlwind of activity arrives, which supports personal growth. You enjoy a bustling and productive time tailor-made for connecting with others who vibrate on a similar wavelength.

4 Saturday ~ Sun square Uranus 2:50

This positive square offers rising creativity that cultivates a new approach. The path ahead clears, and you see improvement flowing into your life. It helps you take those essential steps necessary to expand your life. A new approach begins to prominence, which offers a brighter outlook as it draws vitality into your surroundings. Creating space for more stability draws balance into your world.

5 Sunday ~ Venus square Mars 3:28, Snow Full Moon in Leo 18:30

This square can cause challenges as a difference of opinion fosters tension and conflict. Being flexible, understanding, and adaptive will help harmonize bonds and limit the disruption caused by Venus facing Mars at a harsh angle. Being willing to compromise will improve the foundations and limit the disruption in your life. When you focus on goodness, it has the added benefit of dialing down stress and anxiety.

FEBRUARY

6 Monday ~ Mercury sextile Neptune 18:27

Rational thinking and dreams align in this sextile. You see rising creativity and analytical thinking promoting epiphanies that count. This cosmic alignment helps your dreams become a reality as structured backing behind your vision offers tangible results. An influential person gets involved in encouraging your creativity. Listening to guidance helps shift your focus, keeping life busy with new options and endeavors.

7 Tuesday

News arrives, which brightens the landscape ahead. It lights a path forward that releases outworn areas. It lets you create strides in improving the foundations in your world. It gives you a chance to expand your borders and head toward growth in your social life. Releasing limiting beliefs draws refreshing options that open into a journey ripe for growing. A richer life experience emerges as you schedule fun and engaging activities with friends.

8 Wednesday ~ Venus sextile Uranus 5:28

Spontaneity, fun, and fresh adventures rule your social life with this engaging sextile. It lets you make a splash in a new area. As you debut your talents to a broader audience, you discover new friends and companions who bring engagement and liveliness to your social life. It helps counter stir-crazy feelings, and this has you expressing your wanderlust in a refreshing arena. Rays of sunshine come over the horizon, letting you dip your toes in new adventures.

9 Thursday

Lively discussions nurture well-being and happiness. New options light up across the board, supporting advancement in your life. Changing circumstances brings time for developing goals. Being open to growing your social life brings stability and nurtures well-being. It opens the path to a brighter chapter ahead. It brings a time that rejuvenates your soul as you ride a wave of hopeful energy towards rising prospects.

FEBRUARY

10 Friday ~ Mercury conjunct Pluto 17:16

Today's conjunct between Mercury and Pluto offers intense curiosity to delve a little deeper into life's mysteries. It captures the essence of developing a journey that speaks to your soul. Indeed, you have latent abilities that are tangibly seeking expression. The more you work with your gifts, the more you reveal your inherent skills. It begins a positive trend that marks a new beginning. It emphasizes advancing your abilities.

11 Saturday ~ Mercury ingress Aquarius 11:22

Your willingness to meet new people brings rising prospects into your life. It gives you the chance to reinvent yourself and pour your energy into developing meaningful social bonds. Sharing time with your circle of friends holds the key to growth. It puts you on the path to improving the foundations of your life. It jumpstarts an active time of socializing that connects with your community. Lively discussions relieve stress and offer ideas for future development.

12 Sunday

A change of scene is on the horizon that hits the ticket for rising prospects. It brings a favorable aspect that reboots potential in your world. Your willingness to seek solutions brings new options that let you head towards growth. It enables you to welcome a fresh start that nurtures stability and draws a compelling journey forward in your life. It allows you to touch down on a promising path that facilitates developing your social life.

FEBRUARY

13 Monday ~ Last Quarter Moon in Scorpio 16:01

Significant changes ahead connect you with a prosperous chapter. It offers benefits that shine a light on an expansive and optimistic time of growth in your life. As you develop unique goals that center around your gifts and talents, you promote creativity and amplify the potential possible in your world. It lifts the lid on an inspiring journey that offers a wellspring of goodness. You reawaken to the rich landscape of potential outside your door.

14 Tuesday ~ Valentine's Day

Rising prospects give you the green light to expand your romantic life. Delays that prevented progress no longer cause issues. It is a fantastic time to initiate new plans and improve your love life. Conversations and discussions ahead bring an active environment that fuels bonding—fun and companionship light up harmony in your world. Developing your personal life becomes a strong focus.

15 Wednesday ~ Venus conjunct Neptune 12:25

Venus joins forces with Neptune, and your love life takes on a dreamy quality as you engage in fanciful thoughts and contemplation. The desire moves into unlimited imagination as you think about the future, intending to nurture romance in your life. A sense of wanderlust drives your vision as you chart a course towards exploring new leads. The way ahead is bright and optimistic as you get busy building a journey that holds significant meaning.

16 Thursday ~ Saturn conjunct Sun 16:48

Saturn connects with the Sun to blaze a trail towards developing your goals. Getting serious about limiting distractions and cultivating discipline, concentration, and order will help you nail progress in your working life. Gaining traction on improving the security in your world will bring a valuable sense of achievement and accomplishment to your door. It extends your reach into new areas and attracts many possibilities that tempt you forward.

February

17 Friday

A fresh cycle beckons; the time is right to move forward and head towards expansion in your life. You are ready to engage with the broader world of potential. Serendipity lights the way towards a social aspect that brings new friends and companions into your world. It shines a light on friendship and happiness. Opportunities to engage with your circle of friends get lively discussions and a practical sense of well-being.

18 Saturday ~ Mercury sextile Jupiter 2:13, Sun ingress Pisces 22:30

The Mercury Jupiter aspect creates harmony between both planets. It sparks rising curiosity, questioning, and fresh ideas. It offers a productive environment that lets you carve out a path that offers progression. It heightens confidence, and this is a boost to morale as you discover life becomes more stable. You lift the shutters on an enterprising area that orients a forward-facing journey. Choices and decisions ahead take you towards an ambitious area.

19 Sunday ~ Venus sextile Pluto 17:04

Today's Venus and Pluto alignment offers depth and insight into your thought processes. It helps you dig a little deeper and discover what drives your passion. Thinking about the areas that hold the most significant meaning in your life can be helpful on many levels. It weeds out the areas that no longer are a good fit for your life by letting you see the most meaningful aspects of your world. Moving in alignment with the person you are becoming nurtures inspiration and passion.

February

20 Monday ~ Presidents' Day. New Moon in Pisces 7:08, Venus ingress Aries 7:52

You are on the proper track to improving your life. Getting involved with developing your social life brings stable foundations that grow your vision. An emphasis on improving your life draws fruitful results. A fantastic journey blossoms under your planning and willingness to connect with others who support your life. Opportunities to mingle open your world and expand your horizons.

21 Tuesday ~ Shrove Tuesday (Mardi Gras), Mercury square Uranus 22:22

Original thinking, creative brainstorming, and insightful epiphanies are the order of the day as Mercury squares off against Uranus today. Newfound opportunities roll into your world and connect you with a positive influence. The essence of fate and destiny blend and bring an aspect of synchronicity that sparks your intuition. Expanding your life brings considerable rewards and a chance to forge a friendship.

22 Wednesday ~ Ash Wednesday, Lent Begins, Mercury trine Mars 20:14

A Mercury trine Mars aspect attracts a restless vibe. This cosmic alignment leaves you feeling spontaneous and ready for new adventures today. Life holds a refreshing twist as you begin a time of expansion. Delays and limitations soon lift, drawing improvement into your social life. Staying open to new opportunities brings a busy time of social engagement and companionship. It lightens the load and delivers a wellspring of abundance.

23 Thursday

You reveal information that illuminates a new path. It helps you push back boundaries and make strides toward beginning a new chapter in your life. It refuels emotional and motivational tanks. It brings a beautiful picture of what is possible when you believe in yourself. It helps you grow and develop new areas. It takes confidence and creativity to crack the code of transforming your life.

FEBRUARY

24 Friday

Some unexpected news arrives out of the blue as life heads towards an upswing. New possibilities ahead draw lighter energy around your social life. It offers a highly productive phase that brings chances to socialize and network. You attract more excellent stability, which improves the building blocks of your life. Lively discussions nurture enterprising ideas that spark potential for collaborations.

25 Saturday

Social engagement becomes a focal point as you soon trigger opportunities to mingle. A social environment promotes lively discussions, bringing new options to your table. Your ability to attract positive outcomes is rising as the essence of manifestation stirs up exciting possibilities. Stimulating conversations offer unique ideas, leading to developing a group enterprise. Developments arise that see life become more connected and robust.

26 Sunday

A positive influence sweeps into your life and illustrates a heightened sense of security. It brings a focus on nurturing well-being and harmony on the home front. Getting back to basics tones down stress levels and opens a theme of improving circumstances. It helps you adapt to the broader changes surrounding your life as you progress forward and head towards developing new goals that catch your eye.

March

Sun	Mon	Tue	Wed	Thu	Fri	Sat
			1	2	3	4
5	6	7	8	9	10	11
12	13	14	15	16	17	18
19	20	21	22	23	24	25
26	27	28	29	30	31	

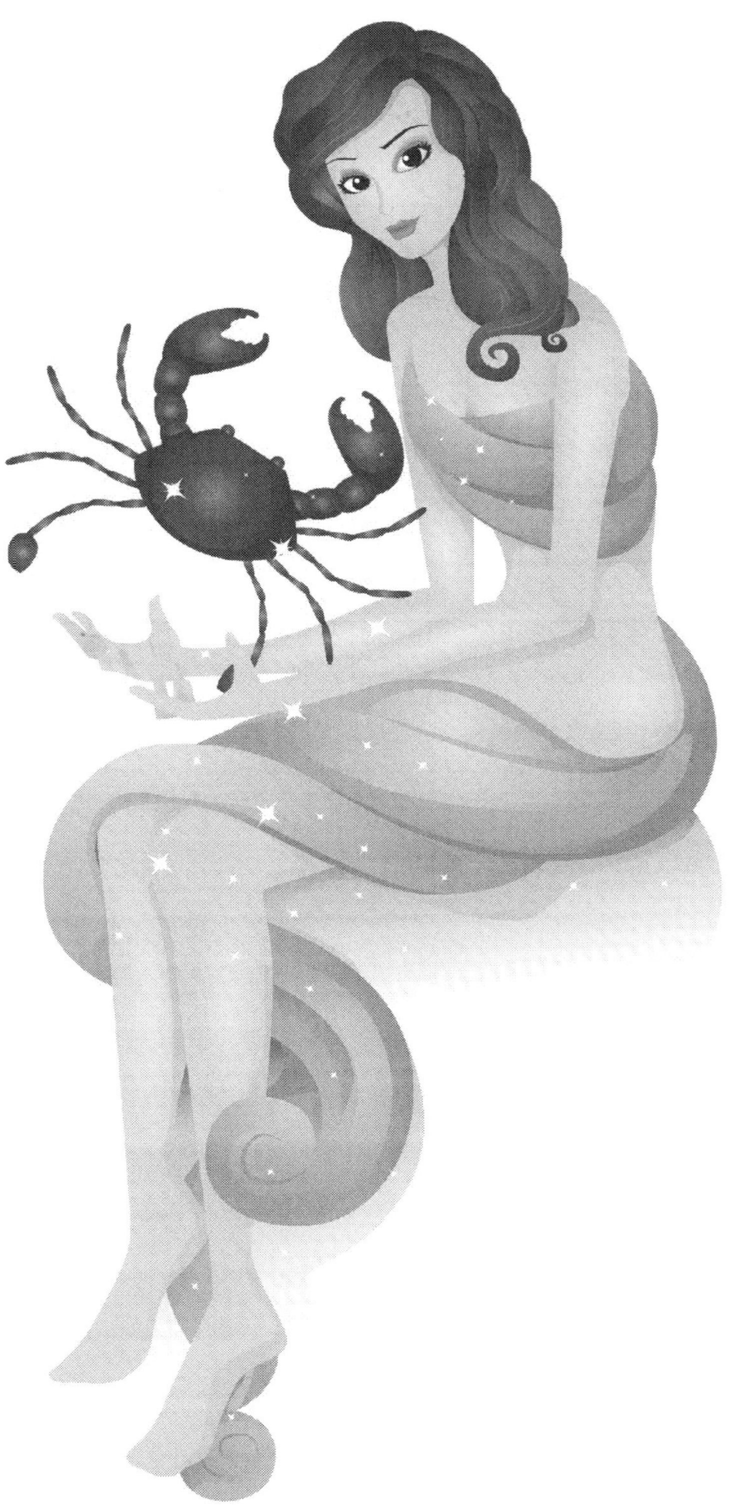

New Moon

WORM MOON

February/March

27 Monday ~ First Quarter Moon in Gemini 8:06

Life heads to an upswing as you transition to a favorable cycle that helps you amplify your vision for future growth. It brings a more active environment that lets you blaze through developing goals. Channeling your energy on a higher level aids the magic of manifestation in your world. Little stands between you and your chosen destination. As you nurture your abilities, you advance towards golden outcomes.

28 Tuesday

Getting back to basics will help restore stable foundations in your life. Prioritizing your goals helps light creativity and artistic expression pathways. Getting involved with areas that offer growth, learning, and advancement helps build stable foundations which kickstart a new enterprise. As you move towards a fresh start, you discover new options ahead that tempt you onwards. The conditions are right to expand your life and head towards a time of growth.

1 Wednesday

You can move forward and bring goodness into your life by being open to new possibilities. Information ahead lets you switch gears and try your talents in a new area. Dipping your skills into the pot of potential brings a growth-orientated phase. A focus on advancement elevates your skills and grows your abilities. It sets the right foundations from which to expand your world.

2 Thursday ~ Venus conjunct Jupiter 17:35, Mercury conjunct Saturn 14:34, Mercury ingress Pisces 22:49

Today's Venus conjunct Jupiter aspect is a positive sign for your social life. Expect an upward trend as rising prospects draw communication and invitations to mingle. It leads to an adventurous trail of lively conversations that are thoughtful and well-meaning. It brings a sense of connection to your world that draws abundance.

MARCH

3 Friday

Life will become attractive as invitations bring a more connected aspect into your life. It shines a light on sharing with your broader circle of friends. Being open to change underscores your willingness to expand horizons and head towards new adventures with companions who offer an engaging pace of life. A positive influence elevates potential and brings rising prospects into your social life.

4 Saturday

You land in an environment that propels you forward, bringing an active socializing time. It offers the perfect backdrop for stepping out into a community setting. It brings a time of new horizons that push back the boundaries and expands your life. A new friendship brings to light, which helps you get involved with opportunities to mingle. It sees a situation blossoming with someone who sparks your curiosity and interest.

5 Sunday

You can pull back when life becomes chaotic. Focusing on the building blocks of your world draws improvement. It helps bring growth into your life as solutions become more apparent when you spend time dabbling in peaceful activities. New goals ahead build on the foundations you create during this time. It turns the leaf into a new chapter that encourages and motivates change.

MARCH

6 Monday ~ Purim (Begins at sundown), Sun sextile Uranus 13:41

This sextile heightens creativity and self-expression. You discover a new approach that boosts productivity and offers efficiency in your daily life. Change and discovery add a spontaneous element today. Anything could crop up to provide you with a sign of newfound inspiration. New options open that tempt you towards growth. It mirrors your desire to improve your situation. It brings a new vibrancy into your world that stirs the coals of your creativity.

7 Tuesday ~ Worm Full Moon in Virgo 12:40 Purim (Ends at sunset), Saturn ingress Pisces 13:03

The planet Saturn moving into Pisces is a significant shift. This changing of the Saturnian guards highlights the need for spiritual healing. It emphasizes finding meaning in your daily life and growing a solid spiritual basis to help you ride out any turbulence in your life. It speaks about stabilizing influences that improve your foundations. It draws renewal and brings support flowing in.

8 Wednesday

You are undergoing a transition that may feel jarring. Taking time to nurture your foundations and focusing on areas that hold meaning in your life draws dividends. You lift the lid on a busy time that helps you gather your resources and prepare for a new chapter of potential. News arrives that brings a piece of sweet information. It offers a considerable boost and hints at a unique journey ahead.

9 Thursday

It's the perfect time to map out new goals for your life. The tides are turning; you can prepare for a positive shift that brings new opportunities into your life. A fork in the road ahead brings a decision; it enables you to build your life in a refreshing direction. It helps remove blocks as you turn the corner and head towards growth. It brings rising creativity to assist in growing your life.

March

10 Friday

Getting involved with developing your talents unearths unique abilities that offer room to grow your world. Your willingness to develop your skills helps you come up with a winning trajectory. It enables you to expand your reach into an enterprising area worth growing. It helps uplift your life on several levels, improves optimism, and brings a more fantastic drive to nail your goals. It soon ratchets up what is possible as you face more significant challenges and growth.

11 Saturday ~ Venus sextile Mars 15:04, Mercury sextile Uranus 21:04

Venus has your back today and draws social engagement into your life. A breakthrough ahead rains new possibilities over your world. It brings refreshing talks with companions who nurture interpersonal bonds, and these discussions offer a more social and dynamic environment. It brings contact with people to grow your circle of friends. It gets a boost as growth moves into your social life. It kicks off a journey that draws improvement and a clear path forward.

12 Sunday

Something percolating in the background of your life will soon appear to point the right path forward. You have undergone many changes recently, leaving you feeling out of sorts. Immersing yourself in the building blocks gets you back to basics and grounds your energy in a helpful area. It creates a balanced and stable environment from which to nurture your dreams. It culminates in a pathway that promotes well-being and draws abundance to your surroundings.

MARCH

13 Monday

It is a time of significant personal growth in your life, and you are on track to expand the borders of your world. Transformation sweeps in to encourage expansion and growth. It lifts the barriers that limit progress as you broaden your world by being open to change. A gateway ahead brings a journey of new adventures. Your intuition guides this process, and you feel drawn to developing a path that reveals hidden depths in your abilities.

14 Tuesday

Contemplating the path ahead helps nurture new options. Doing due diligence lets you proactively engage with developing your career path. It launches a journey towards an area that holds promise. Focusing on your priorities spells out the stepping stones that will take you towards advancement. As you break down the limitations, you discover that opportunity comes knocking. News arrives that brings a boost to your spirit.

15 Wednesday ~ Last Q Moon in Sagittarius 2:08, Sun conjunct Neptune 23:39

You may feel sensitivities rising today as the Sun links up with Neptune in the sign of Pisces today. Intuition is sparking, and you can trust your gut instincts to guide you correctly when you reveal curious information that triggers your emotions. Let your feelings out as you embrace nurturing your true potential. Being open to change helps you pass the threshold and enter a brighter, happier chapter ahead.

16 Thursday ~ Mercury conjunct Neptune 17:13, Sun square Mars 18:09, Venus square Pluto 19:58, Venus ingress Taurus 22:31

Today, you may feel chaotic and under pressure as a great deal of cosmic energy disrupts stability in your life. Expect intensity as the Sun square Mars alignment may leave you tense and hot under the collar. Creative expression and taking time to make yourself a priority will be beneficial in releasing frustrations and any heavy energy clinging to your spirit.

MARCH

**17 Friday ~ St Patrick's Day. Mercury square Mars 4:48,
Sun conjunct Mercury 10:45, Venus sextile Saturn 20:25**

Today, Venus sextile Saturn promotes cooperation and offers the chance to join a joint project. You connect with someone who operates on a similar wavelength. It draws well-being and companionship into your world. It lights a path that offers growth, prosperity, and abundance. It lets you merge creative ideas that provide an opportunity for collaboration.

18 Saturday

A new chapter arrives that flips the switch on a more social environment. It is a carefree and happy time that lets you relax and unwind with friends. Networking with your tribe brings opportunities for collaboration. It gives you a chance to develop a creative aspect that grows your talents. Nurturing your gifts brings an expansive chapter that cultivates growth in your life. It brings a lively time that draws happiness into your world.

19 Sunday ~ Mercury ingress Aries 4:22

You hone in on an exciting new chapter and receive a wind of refreshing potential that inspires change. Expanding your horizons, reshuffle the decks of fate. It correlates with plenty of new energy coming into your social life. It transitions to a more social environment that tempts you forward. The path ahead glimmers with possibilities. It sets the stage for a journey that offers growth and rising prospects in your life.

MARCH

20 Monday ~ Sun sextile Pluto 20:12, Sun ingress Aries 21:20, Ostara/Spring Equinox 21:25

Changes ahead bring movement and discovery into your world. Serendipity lights the path forward as destiny calls your name. Being flexible helps you pivot away from problematic areas that no longer bear fruit. Intelligent decisions ahead place you in the correct alignment to grow your world. You connect with an adviser who offers support and wisdom.

21 Tuesday ~ New Moon in Pisces 17:22

Doing your own thing sets the stage for developing working goals. It lets you set your sights on an impressive avenue that plants the seeds to grow into something spectacular. Your attention to detail and your willingness to work towards your vision nurture a dynamic environment. It helps you breeze through an active phase and enjoy a lighter and happier phase of building stable foundations in the workplace.

22 Wednesday ~ Ramadan Begins

News arrives that earmarks a new beginning for your life. It brings an active and progressive chapter that offers a shift forward towards developing new goals. It brings a window of opportunity that helps get life back on track with endeavors that capture your interest. Opening the gates wide to these possibilities shines a light on a happy and abundant landscape. Being open to change facilitates growth; it allows you to grow your abilities and work with your talents.

23 Thursday ~ Pluto ingress Aquarius 8:42

An opportunity arrives that lights a path forward for your working life. It draws an essential time for advancing goals and developing your skills. It nurtures a strong foundation from which to grow your working goals. Exploring your options unearths a genuine lead that brings new responsibilities and prosperity into your world. Exploring options helps you create a strategy that brings success to your table.

March

24 Friday

Life holds a refreshing change as a buzz of activity around your social life brings new possibilities to light. It helps you achieve closure as you feel more optimistic about moving forward. Embracing new experiences and people widens the borders of your life. It draws lighter energy as a fresh wind of possibility tempts you forward. Opportunities to socialize ahead draw fruitful discussions that pave the way to expand your circle of friends.

25 Saturday ~ Mars ingress Cancer 11:36

You glide into the potential that offers a social aspect. It enables you to get more involved with friends and acquaintances. It emphasizes developing bonds that provide room to grow your social life. It brings the chance to unwind with friends and kindred spirits. It helps you release your troubles and reconnects you to what is vital for your soul. It brings the green light to cherish and engage with your social circle.

26 Sunday

It is a time of change that lets you make a breakthrough ahead. It connects you with potential that improves your prospects. It brings a refreshing and lively pace that draws happiness and rewarding outcomes. New possibilities flood your life with options; it keeps you busy with new endeavors and projects to consider. It brings inspiring conversations that give the chance to share trailblazing ideas and thoughts.

MARCH

27 Monday

The choices and decisions ahead drive a vital growth phase into your life. Opportunity comes knocking; it connects you with an avenue worth development. Seeing your circumstances improve gives you the green light to expand your life outwardly. It brings empowering options that let you power through to a brighter chapter. You stand on a rare and exciting precipice of change.

28 Tuesday ~ Mercury conjunct Jupiter 6:49

This astrological conjunct is perfect for brainstorming as ideas are big and expressive under this planetary influence. Your sense of adventure reawakens to a rich landscape of potential that surrounds your life. It takes you on a journey imbued with possibility and excitement. Spending time with kindred spirits feeds the furnace of your inspiration. Clues ahead help you reveal a new option. It brings an assignment that blends perfectly with your aspirations.

29 Wednesday ~ First Quarter Moon in Cancer 2:32

A more stable landscape will emerge soon. It lets you channel your energy productively into an area that offers room for progression. An exciting new landscape draws change overhead. New options arrive that support your vision for growth and abundance. Embracing life-affirming endeavors brings equilibrium and secures a stable and harmonious environment. It expands your life, bringing new possibilities overhead.

30 Thursday ~ Mars trine Saturn 19:03, Venus conjunct Uranus 22:25

Mars forms a trine with Saturn today to give your working life wings. Hard work, dedication, and perseverance improve the day-to-day foundations of your life. Venus teams up with Uranus to add a dash of spontaneity to your social/personal life. As you set out on a new adventure, staying true to yourself will keep you aligned with the person you are becoming. You chart a course towards spending time with friends as you open the door to a new chapter.

April

Sun	Mon	Tue	Wed	Thu	Fri	Sat
						1
2	3	4	5	6	7	8
9	10	11	12	13	14	15
16	17	18	19	20	21	22
23	24	25	26	27	28	29
30						

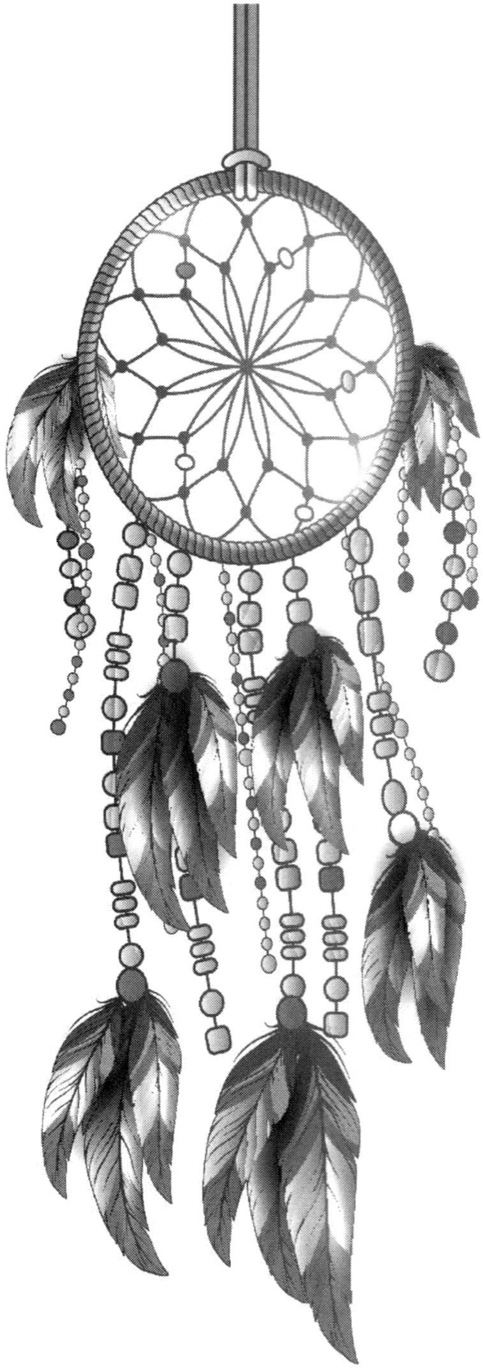

New Moon

Pink Moon

March/April

31 Friday

Curious possibilities ahead ramp up motivation and leave you optimistic about life. It promotes a busy time that sees you gaining traction on developing your life outwardly. Difficulties fade as you rekindle inspiration and turn the corner, heading towards growth. A fantastic opportunity attracts optimism and joy. It brings unexpected developments into your social life that cracks the code to a brighter chapter.

1 Saturday ~ All Fools/April Fool's Day

Changes ahead bring new options into your world. It helps you move forward sustainably, and as things open up, you discover new pathways that grow the potential possible. You soon resolve minor issues and enter an enriching phase that lets you plot a course towards a happier chapter. Social engagement brings lively discussions and a chance to expand your social circle. It does offer the opportunity for a joint venture.

2 Sunday ~ Palm Sunday.

Being open to developing new areas facilitates change which opens your life to an exciting flavor. It ends delays as you find heartening progress that lights the path forward. Your social life blooms under sunny skies. Life has more substance and significance as you concentrate on personal goals that hold the most significant meaning in your life. News arrives that brings an invitation out and about.

April

3 Monday ~ Mercury ingress Taurus 16:20

News arrives that draws a positive influence. It heightens your ability to develop your talents and extend your reach into new areas. Indeed, long-term goals come into focus; essential planning tackles strategy and lets you plot a course towards expansion. It draws an active time that opens your life to a bounty of potential. A new flow of options brings an influx of information. It can take time to process and digest the possibilities.

4 Tuesday

Notable changes ahead highlight a journey of growth and progress in your life. Attractive options bring new possibilities into your life. As motivation increases, you soon feel the lightness returning full force to your energy. It lets you touch down on a path that promotes the development of unique projects that capture the essence of creativity. It attracts a bustling environment that grows your talents and offers advancement.

5 Wednesday ~ Passover (begins at sunset), Mercury sextile Saturn 16:18

With Mercury in sextile with Saturn, communication skills are rising. Enhanced clarity and mental insight help you understand more significant concepts, thought processes, and ideas with ease today. This cosmic enhancement enables you to step beyond traditional or repetitive learning and take your studies/working life to the next level. It helps you rise to the challenge and pole vault successfully over the hump day.

6 Thursday ~ Lent Ends. Pink Full Moon in Libra 4:37

A healing influence surrounds your current situation. This therapeutic aspect helps provide you with a sturdier foundation; it nurtures balance and promotes growth in your life. You find it is suitable for your spirit as it heals old wounds. Attractive options ahead help you move away from sadness. Spending time nurturing your social life brings a winning chapter into view. You attract possibilities that are compatible with your vision for future growth.

APRIL

7 Friday ~ Good Friday, Venus sextile Neptune 17: 59

Today's planetary alignment offers a mindful, spiritual aspect that is in keeping with the spirit of Easter. Venus sends loving beams into your home and family life, harmonizing bonds and drawing the essence of rejuvenation and renewal. Connecting with people you hold near and dear places a focus on well-being and harmony. It directs your attention towards a supportive and nurturing environment that soothes and refreshes your energy and brings cherished moments.

8 Saturday ~ Mercury sextile Mars 6:23

A sextile between Mercury and Mars sharpens cognitive abilities today. Mental clarity is on the rise, giving you valuable insight into the path ahead. It has you thinking about making some changes and moving your skills into a new area. Nurturing creativity lets you rejuvenate your energy and enjoy a refreshing potential landscape. You embark on a journey of developing your talents as destiny comes calling.

9 Sunday ~Easter Sunday

Taking a step back draws a grounded and peaceful environment. It brings a chance to focus on developing stable foundations, bringing a sense of rejuvenation. It helps you pour your energy into a meaningful area key to a growth cycle. Exciting changes ahead bring a remarkable trajectory that lets you get busy and build a bridge towards a brighter future.

April

10 Monday

Sizeable changes ahead crack the code to a brighter chapter. It inspires growth, and being open and flexible in your plans will help you make the most of an energized time ahead. It triggers a highly creative phase where you come up with ideas and develop an innovative approach that enables you to uncover hidden gems of possibility. Change is in the wind; transformational projects take a bold place in your world.

11 Tuesday ~ Venus ingress Gemini 4:43, Venus trine Pluto 10:14, Sun Conjunct Jupiter 22:07, Mercury at Greatest Elong 19.5E

Unique option emerges, which gives you a chance to develop your abilities and grow the path ahead. A strong emphasis on evolving your skills lets you capture the essence of advancement. Things are moving as you head towards a productive and active environment that offers rising prospects. Optimism and inspiration run wild as you embark on developing life in a refreshing direction.

12 Wednesday

You enter a good time to expand your life. It brings a rich offering of new possibilities to tempt you forward. A curious assignment draws excitement and inspiration. It lights a path towards a journey that offers luck and good fortune. Your talents take center stage as you chart a course towards working with your abilities. Growing your skills brings a profitable opportunity that offers gold for your working life.

13 Thursday ~ Passover (ends at sunset), Last Quarter Moon in Capricorn 9:11

You are on a continuous cycle of change and evolution. Life supports developing your vision for future growth. Opportunities crop up, which encourage you to dream big. You move forward with confidence, and acting on your instincts draws a valuable result. Clearing the way the cobwebs offers an open road of potential as you pursue advancing your life into uncharted territory. It opens a time of new beginnings that draws happiness.

April

14 Friday ~ Orthodox Good Friday, Venus square Saturn 16:38

A Venus square Saturn encourages taking a personal inventory of meaningful areas in your life. Adjusting course as necessary will give private bonds the best chance of success. Shining a more intensive light on interpersonal situations in your social life helps you see the truth and cut away from outworn areas. Being clear about things enables you to cut away from toxic influences that limit you from reaching your highest trajectory. Saturn will help you trim the deadwood.

15 Saturday

An exciting new possibility ahead brings a valuable gift into your life. It offers a social aspect that sees you mixing and mingling with friends. It provides ample time for lively discussions that maximize the harmony in your world. You hit the jackpot when you spark innovative conversations with an insightful companion. It brings contentment and happiness into your social life. A sudden breakthrough offers insight into the path ahead that changes your perspective.

16 Sunday ~ Orthodox Easter

It is a time that underscores how important it is to treat yourself. Having some luxury around your life draws well-being and harmony into view. It lights a path that lets you follow your heart and chase your dreams. It brings new projects and endeavors that capture the essence of inspiration. Growing your world extends your talents into new areas, bringing great excitement.

April

17 Monday

Lovely changes flow into your life when news arrives, which speaks of change. An impressive option lets you come out a winner as it brings an engaging and busy chapter ahead. A fruitful outcome on the horizon enables you to blaze a trail towards rising prospects. It kicks off a time of promise and prosperity as you draw advancement and tap into growth pathways. Working with your talents draws dividends and lights up a journey that evolves your skills.

18 Tuesday

Nurturing the foundations in your life brings a balanced and stable environment. New leads emerge that have you thinking about growth. A learning option ahead becomes a source of inspiration. It offers both challenges and progression for your career path. Being open to developing your skills advances life towards greener pastures. It lets you touch down on an extended time of growing your dreams.

19 Wednesday

Life supports your efforts to improve circumstances. New possibilities spark a journey that offers expansion. It shines a light on goals, status, and career success. Putting the finishing touches on your strategy lets you develop a winning trajectory when news arrives that encourages expansion. Rising prospects open up an avenue that offers growth and security. It allows you to move towards advancement.

20 Thursday ~ Ramadan Ends, New Moon in Taurus 4:12, Hybrid Solar Eclipse, Sun ingress Taurus 8:09, Sun square Pluto 16:26

The Sun square Pluto aspect draws renewal and rejuvenation. Pluto charts a course towards transformation and offers a highly creative part that lights the way forward towards improving your circumstances. The Sun contributes golden beings that offer harmony, transcendence, and rising prospects. This planetary combo elevates creative inclinations.

April

21 Friday ~ Mercury turns Retrograde in Taurus at 8:34

Mercury plays havoc with interpersonal bonds and can send communication haywire during its retrograde phase. Buckle up; it will be a bumpy ride as your social life goes on a Mercury-driven rollercoaster. If someone's contact triggers an emotional aspect, be mindful that this planetary phase is best with a balanced and understanding approach. Being adaptable and flexible will give you a solid basis to stabilize personal bonds.

22 Saturday ~ Earth Day, Lyrids Meteor Shower from April 16th -25th

A surprise invitation arrives, bringing excitement and happiness. You feel optimistic about the prospects ahead as it draws a lively chapter into your social life. A new friendship blossoms, and this enriches your world. It brings a time of networking and mingling with others who understand and support your world. Sharing with a valued companion gets a boost.

23 Sunday

New information ahead cracks the code to a brighter chapter. It opens the gate to a fresh start which marks the beginning of a remarkable journey. An area you nurture blossoms into a meaningful path forward for your social life. It connects you with others on a similar trajectory and willing to support your world with thoughtful discussions and opportunities to mingle. Sharing with valued companions promotes well-being and happiness.

APRIL

24 Monday ~ Mercury sextile Mars 3:22

Quick reflexes enable you to spot the diamond in the rough. The Mercury sextile with Mars offers new leads. Something special makes a grand entrance into your life; transformation and expansion soon follow. You discover a beautiful symmetry is involved as life comes full circle. A treasure trove of possibilities cranks up the inspiration and has you daydreaming about the possibilities.

25 Tuesday ~ Sun sextile Saturn 10:47

Today's sextile brings opportunities that light a path forward. It illuminates fantastic potential that enables you to improve your circumstances. Dissolving barriers and embracing a newfound sense of lightness brings enthusiasm into your working life. You get involved in an active and productive environment. Gathering your resources, you undertake the work necessary and enjoy a busy time.

26 Wednesday

You benefit from new opportunities that take you towards a refreshing chapter. Creativity is rising, and this encourages growth and learning. If you have felt as though you are standing at a crossroads, a decision you make turns out to be a winner. You unleash possibilities that kick off a stable phase of advancement. It draws security that lays the correct foundation for your home life. Provides a secure link that helps you forge a unique path ahead.

27 Thursday ~ First Quarter Moon in Leo 21:20

Exciting new energy flows into your world, bringing change. It kickstarts an expressive phase that offers renewal and rejuvenation. It opens the doors to a journey that brings social engagement and happiness. Sharing with kindred spirits brings brainstorming sessions that provide opportunities for collaboration. It brings newfound motivation that fuels expansion in your life.

April

28 Friday

A new vision takes shape as the path ahead glitters with golden opportunities. It brings an essential time for advancing goals and developing an area of interest. It taps into a creative vibe that cracks the code to rising prospects. A refreshing change of pace ahead opens the gate to new adventures. An emphasis on developing your social life brings a winning chapter into view.

29 Saturday ~ Mars sextile Uranus 8:04

This sextile brings unique ideas that help you think outside the box to obtain innovative solutions. Uranus places the focus on rebellion, liberation, and freedom. Events line up beautifully to nourish your soul as you expand the borders of your world. It brings a sense of fun and excitement as you fling open the doors and enjoy a sunny aspect overhead. It lightens the load and delivers a wellspring of abundance, allowing you to reawaken to a rich landscape of possibility.

30 Sunday

A refreshing change of pace helps break old patterns and ways of thinking. It takes you on a journey of new horizons which spark movement and discovery. Growing and expanding your social life improves the building blocks of stability. A new approach brings companionship and lively discussions which spark creative ideas. Life soon becomes more expressive and connected.

May

Sun	Mon	Tue	Wed	Thu	Fri	Sat
	1	2	3	4	5	6
7	8	9	10	11	12	13
14	15	16	17	18	19	20
21	22	23	24	25	26	27
28	29	30	31			

AQUARIUS
VIRGO TAURUS
SCORPIO MARS STARS SUN
ARIES CAPRICORN WEDDING WEALTH FORTUNE
CALENDAR
GEMINI LOVE ASTROLOGY
MOON MONTH
LEO HOROSCOPE
SAGITTARIUS HAPPINESS
BIRTHDAY ASTRONOMY
CANCER LIBRA NEPTUNE DATE ZODIAC
PISCES SKY EARTH SIGN
TODAY DAILY WEEKLY
CONSTELLATION MONTHLY

New Moon

Flower Moon

May

1 Monday ~ Beltane/May Day, Pluto turns retrograde in Aquarius 18:39, Sun conjunct Mercury 23:27

Pluto is the modern ruler of Scorpio; it symbolizes how we experience power, renewal, rebirth, and mysterious or subconscious forces. This retrograde phase lasts until October. It allows you to dive deep and explore inner realms and darker aspects of your personality ordinarily hidden from view. Understanding your psyche on a deeper level provides access to the forces driving your personality. It lets you comprehend the why and wherefore behind desires.

2 Tuesday

A lucrative offer brings a bonus into your life. It governs a phase of progression that helps you create those lifestyle changes that have been on the back burner for some time. It draws security and releases troublesome energy; you discover an efficient way to progress towards your vision. Something out of the blue arrives and offers an assignment you can sink your teeth into developing. It draws a project that inspires your mind.

3 Wednesday

Your career path does exceedingly well and brings an innovative and productive time. Learning the intricacies of a new venture lets you reach new standards in the workplace. You have the discipline to stick with goals and achieve a pleasing outcome. It does allow you to dream big and navigate around obstacles with finesse. An offshoot or side venture comes calling and may bring something worth building as a sideline.

4 Thursday ~ Venus square Neptune 17:40

A Venus square Neptune aspect offers a dreamy quality. It provides the perfect vibe for engaging in the big sky dreaming about your perfect romantic escapade. While fairytales in the sky offer relaxation and escapism, it's important to remember that this dreaminess could lead to delusion if you overly focus on something currently out of reach. Understanding the escapism and creative elements at play enables you to dream big and still feel grounded in reality.

MAY

5 Friday ~ Venus sextile Jupiter 4:02, Flower Full Moon in Scorpio 17:34 Penumbral Lunar Eclipse

Venus and Jupiter's sextile create beneficial and harmonious vibrations. Good luck and rising prospects bring warmth and social engagement. Creating space to nurture your social life draws possibilities to light. You get busy crafting with friends and enjoy a vibrant chapter that ushers in invitations and opportunities to mingle. It brings the sort of connection that feels supportive and engaging.

6 Saturday ~ Eta Aquarids Meteor Shower April 19th - May 28th

The scene ahead sets a lively chapter. It places you in the proper alignment to improve your social life. It brings opportunities to connect with others, and this support becomes something you treasure. It brings an ally who shares discussions and thoughts that inspire your mind. It takes you towards expansion and opportunity. It brings a newfound sense of confidence that lets you step boldly onto a new path.

7 Sunday ~ Venus ingress Cancer 14:20

Events on the horizon will beautifully support you. It lights a path of kinship and social involvement. It does keep your schedule busy and active. New possibilities let you dive deep into a productive chapter. It brings a beautiful journey that advances your circumstances. Investigating your options brings leads that inspire expansion. Your friends and contacts play a role in this journey.

MAY

8 Monday

When news arrives, a fresh cycle beckons, inspiring growth around your working goals. It helps you release old patterns that block progress. It grows your ambitious side as it offers advancement. It reawakens you to what is possible when you extend your reach and dive into an empowering chapter of increasing your career dreams. Setting goals and creating plans draws fruitful results.

9 Tuesday ~ Sun conjunct Uranus 19:55

Something important appears in your life and marks a bold debut. It does let you distance yourself from drama, and as you shed this outworn skin, a new priority comes into focus. It does bring a journey that offers unique experiences, friendships, and possibilities. The fires of your inspiration burn brightly, igniting a personal goal. It lets you strike gold and turn the corner on a winning chapter.

10 Wednesday

Opportunity comes knocking as curious changes ahead bring an improvement of circumstances to your door. It ushers in a time of refreshing possibilities that helps you make strides in advancing your goals. It emphasizes developing your working life as you find new challenges to sink your teeth into producing. A buzz of excitement brings new possibilities to light that inspire learning and growth. It redefines what you thought was possible in your working life.

11 Thursday

A shift ahead lets you uncover a journey that helps you create balanced and stable foundations. As you paint the backdrop to this canvas of dreams, you begin to fill in the finer details of where this journey leads. Little goes under your radar as you spot the right environment from which to grow your world. A golden aspect weaves around your creativity and enables you to chart a course towards developing your vision for future growth.

MAY

12 Friday ~ Mercury sextile Saturn 8:32, Last Quarter Moon in Aquarius 14:28

Mercury sextile Saturn gives your Friday a boost which helps you tidy up loose ends before the weekend. Mental acuity rises, bringing a focused mind and increased powers of observation lets you see what needs addressing. Today's other cognitive improvements include excellent concentration, memory, and organization skills. With everything running smoothly in your working life, you can enjoy the weekend ahead knowing you have taken care of business.

13 Saturday ~ Mercury sextile Venus 2:41, Venus trine Saturn 6:56

Mercury sextile Venus offers a social and friendly influence making this a great day to connect with your tribe. An invitation ahead lets you treat yourself to a relaxing and engaging time shared with friends. You get the right kind of attention when others reach out to organize a catch-up. It brings the type of conversations to map out ideas and plan for future growth. It creates a bridge between your burgeoning creativity and tangible results.

14 Sunday ~ Mother's Day (US)

You stake your claim on a basket of good fortune that promises to deliver excellent results. It helps you make a move towards improving your home life. Sound foundations and draw rising stability which nurtures greater security in your life. An area you become involved with developing initiates transformation. It rekindles vitality as growing creativity helps you think outside the box and find new possibilities ahead.

May

15 Monday ~ Mercury turns direct in Taurus 3:16, Mars trine Neptune 13:44

With Mercury turning direct today, the focus is on your social life. Mars forms a trine with Neptune, enhancing potential as confidence rises and you feel ready for social engagement. It offers the perfect solution for the doldrums as you get busy being self-expressive, communicative, and creative. It provides a freedom-driven chapter that helps you make the most of your rebellious energy. It gives an area to channel your excess power into to embrace socializing with friends.

16 Tuesday ~ Jupiter ingress Taurus 17:01

You land in a new and exciting landscape as essential changes ahead bring expansion and growth. Focusing on the building blocks helps you make the right moves that progress your situation forward. It lets you set off on a new adventure that nurtures your inspiration and draws happiness into your life. It connects you with like-minded people, and social interaction draws well-being and harmony.

17 Wednesday

News arrives that cracks the code to a brighter chapter in your life. You discover endless possibilities due to your willingness to be open to exploring unique leads. It opens a time of nurturing social connections and drawing well-being into your world. A shift forward offers a richly abundant journey that blesses your spirit. It shines a light on an expressive and optimistic environment that promotes companionship. It lifts the lid on a promising social engagement.

18 Thursday ~ Jupiter square Pluto 1:09, Sun sextile Neptune 8:59

Today's Jupiter square Pluto brings extra drive and increased energy to complete projects and finish your to-do list. Neptune also boosts your goals as a sextile with the Sun helps you find the resources and support needed to manifest your vision. You can bring your dreams to reality as the planets have your back today, attracting rising prospects into your life. It shines a light on developing your career as your efforts draw momentum.

MAY

19 Friday ~ Mercury sextile Saturn 6:50 New Moon in Taurus 15:54

Today, Mercury, Saturn sextile boosts your communication skills and confidence. Add in a dash of New Moon inspiration and aspiration. You have the perfect mix for engaging in brainstorming with valued companions. Sharing ideas and adding creative ingredients into the pot of manifestation helps you develop a winning trajectory from which to grow your world.

20 Saturday ~ Mars ingress Leo 15:24

Mars lands in Leo, and this raises confidence. It's time to go big and be proud and bold. A great deal of potential takes you towards a phase of expansion, prosperity, and growth. It brings a venture that captures your interest. This area gives you a chance to develop an endeavor that inspires your mind. It is a good time when you take steps toward progressing your goals. There is plenty to celebrate; a gathering of friends brings lively discussions.

21 Sunday ~ Mars opposed Pluto 3:11, Sun ingress Gemini 7:04, Sun trine Pluto 13:58

Mars connects with a competitive edge today that could see your authority tested. The Sun trine Pluto aspect also adds fuel to the fire as it increases your desire to gain power and feed your ambitious streak. You seek opportunities to elevate your standing among peers and co-workers today. Climbing the ladder towards success becomes a dominant factor.

MAY

22 Monday ~ Victoria Day (Canada), Sun sextile Mars 5:56

The Sun sextile Mars transit brings vital energy and renewed zest for life. It's time to move forward and grow your dreams and goals. A cascade of new possibilities arrives to break down the barriers that prevent progress. It creates a wildfire of creativity that stimulates innovative solutions and progress in your life. Your dedication and commitment draw dividends.

23 Tuesday ~ Mars square Jupiter 5:13

Today's Mars square Jupiter offers a positive influence that increases stamina and boosts your energy. Enthusiasm for the task at hand rises, boosting productivity and enabling you to deal with the day's demands efficiently and capably. Marching to the beat of your drum cracks the code to an ample time. As the axis of your life shifts, it draws your attention forward, which emphasizes the expansion that launches your ship of dreams.

24 Wednesday

During this valuable time, shifting into builder mode lets you progress your concepts and create tangible forms of your ideas. The time is ripe for projects and endeavors as you soon kick off a prosperous chapter of initiating new ventures. It is a powerful time for manifesting; an area you get off the ground soon takes shape. You enter a purposeful time of using your talents to achieve pleasing results. Performance is rising, drawing accolades and success.

25 Thursday ~ Shavuot (Begins at sunset)

A social aspect ahead puts fresh wind in your sails. It brings a time of lively discussions and stimulating conversations that promote creativity. A leap of faith broadens horizons and marks the beginning of a journey that attracts a pleasing outcome. Sharing with friends adds a dash of spice and excitement that brings new flavors into your social life. It underscores the energy of magic that surrounds your world as the borders of your life dissolve.

May

26 Friday ~ Venus sextile Uranus 7:36

Today's sextile promotes a vibrant and active social life. With Venus charming and Uranus adding a dash of spontaneity to your weekend plans, it assures a fun and lively time shared with friends. A time of growth ahead brings soul-expanding experiences with kindred spirits. It brings rock-solid foundations that give you a new start that improves your circumstances. Goals and dreams take flight under the winds of momentum that flow into your world.

27 Saturday ~ Shavuot (Ends at sunset), First Quarter Moon in Virgo 15:22

New ideas and press information pave the way forward. It brings a life-changing chapter that holds enticing potential for your social life. A situation you become involved with begins to move forward; it draws lighter energy that offers expansion and growth. You deepen a bond with a person who helps you thrive. It is a time that reshapes your social life and encourages change that ramps up the potential possible. It draws a harmonious phase of engagement and joy.

28 Sunday

Lively discussions with friends and companions spark a promising chapter in your social life. Curious news arrives that offers insight into an engaging and happy time ahead. It opens the floodgates to socialize with your broader circle of friends. It shines a light on an active and dynamic chapter that helps you establish greener pastures in your life. The winds of change breathe fresh possibilities that motivate and inspire you greatly in your life.

JUNE

Sun	Mon	Tue	Wed	Thu	Fri	Sat
				1	2	3
4	5	6	7	8	9	10
11	12	13	14	15	16	17
18	19	20	21	22	23	24
25	26	27	28	29	30	

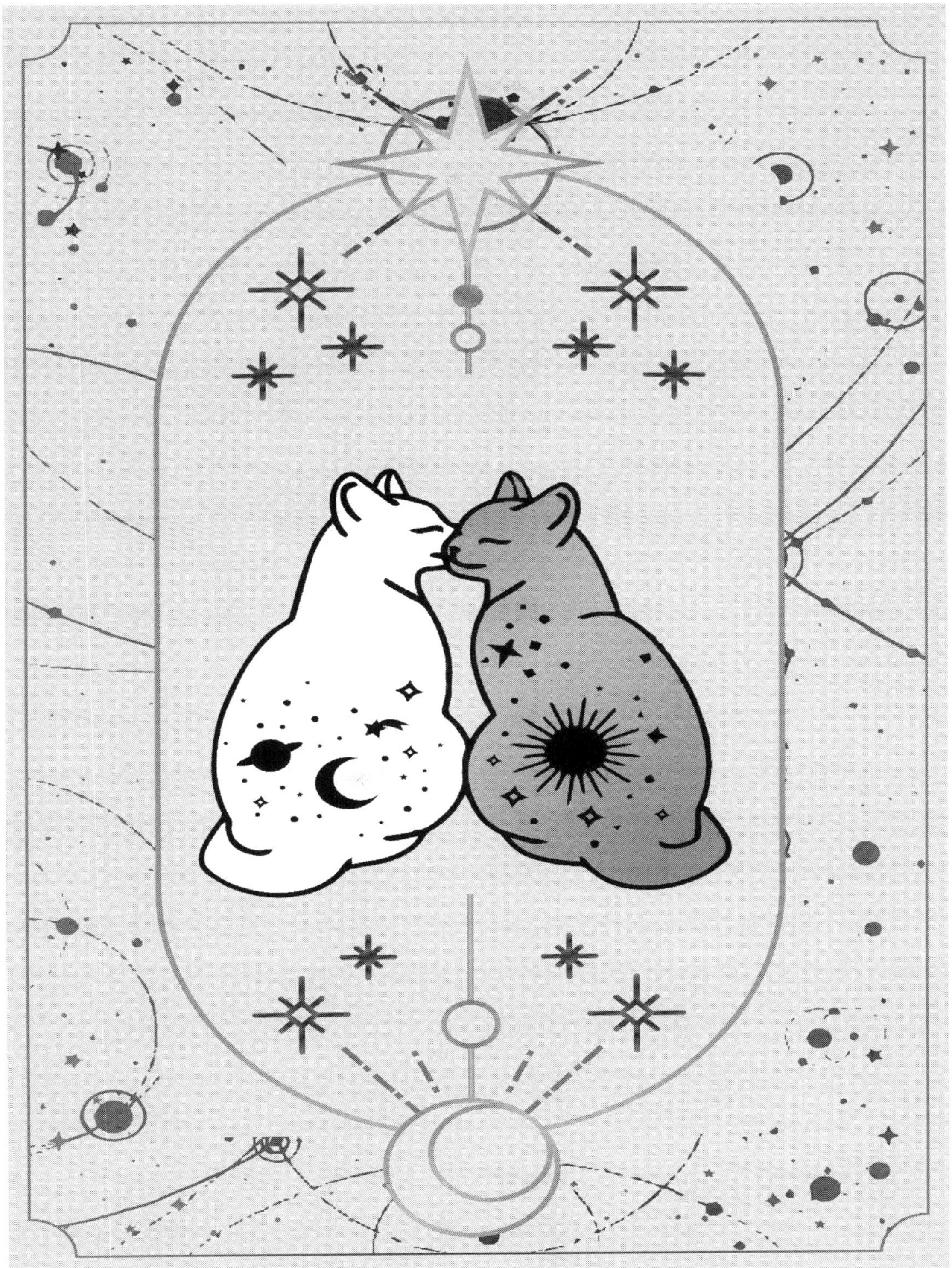

New Moon

Strawberry Moon

May/June

29 Monday ~ Memorial Day, Mercury at Greatest Elongation 24.9W

A lighter flow of energy emerges in your world soon. It brings sunny skies overhead that connect you with a social aspect that enriches your life. You launch into a time of mingling with people, developing new projects, and chasing potential leads. Additionally, one old friend is keen to reconnect with you. Spending time with this person is a source of great happiness and joy.

30 Tuesday

A curious assignment comes along that gives you the motivation to expand your horizons. It triggers an exciting path that lays the groundwork for future progress. Refining your talents and working with your abilities brings new information to light. Your efforts soon bear fruit, making it the ideal time to take on a new area of interest. It brings the prize of harmony into your world.

31 Wednesday

You receive news that brings an unexpected opportunity to your door that offers a new assignment. It brings advancement and recognition to your career path. It gets a chance to take on more responsibilities and head towards growth. It draws a busy and productive time for growing your career prospects. As you climb the ladder towards success, it brings robust and steady progression into view.

1 Thursday

New foundations are ahead that bring a positive aspect to light. Refreshing options encourage expansion, and being actively involved in growing your world lets you move towards an abundant chapter. It brings a fantastic time that clears the decks and draws new possibilities into your social life. You make waves as you chase a unique aspect that lights up pathways of inspiration and excitement.

June

2 Friday ~ Venus trine Neptune 22:42

Creativity and imagination are peaking under the blissful Venus, Neptune trine. Harmony, equilibrium, and well-being soar under this positive influence. Self-expression is rising, cultivating a unique path that captures the essence of artistic inclinations. Venus showers positivity over your social life, improving personal bonds. It leads to an uplifting time discussing future projects and endeavors with a kindred spirit who understands your mindset and outlook on life.

3 Saturday

Information ahead connects you with a chapter of fun and adventure. It brings a time that brims with potential as you scope out a path that offers room to engage with life. Channeling your creative energy into an area that resonates with possibility sees fortune turning in your favor. It takes you on a journey that offers growth, learning, and advancement. It offers a busy and active chapter that draws lively discussions and stimulating conversations with kindred spirits.

4 Sunday ~ Strawberry Full Moon in Sagittarius 3:42, Mercury conjunct Uranus 19:50

Mercury and Uranus form a positive aspect that heightens mental abilities. Increasing mental stimulation promotes fresh ideas in your life today. Technology, messages, and communication all play a part in sparking inspiration and fostering possibilities for future development. It brings a burst of inspiration, an opportunity that breathes new life into your foundations.

June

5 Monday ~ Venus ingress Leo 13:42, Venus opposed Pluto 16:04

Your career path heats up when sudden developments arrive to shake up the potential possible. It draws advancement and change that has the potential to re-invent your situation. The time is right for chasing dreams and embracing a journey of growth and prosperity. After the destabilizing times of recent months, you find your feet in a landscape ripe for progression. It helps initiate a positive chapter that carries you forward.

6 Tuesday

Exploring different pathways help you find out who you are on a deeper level. Taking responsibility for your personal development lets you move in alignment with your core beliefs. It enables you to align yourself with people who share a similar purpose. It empowers you to lead from an authentic place and learn to trust your instincts. It helps you develop a profound connection with people who resonate on a similar wavelength.

7 Wednesday

A path of higher learning and wisdom calls your name. It brings a chance to develop a journey that aligns with your becoming. You drift away from areas that did not reach fruition; removing the outworn layers helps you embrace new possibilities that flow into your life. News on the horizon brings insight into the path ahead. It begins a hero's journey of expanding your life outwardly.

8 Thursday

You gain some clarity around your situation, which draws peace into your surroundings. It brings insight into the path ahead that helps you release guilt and doubt. It sweeps away outworn energy and creates space to focus on nurturing your dreams. It connects you with others who come in to assist this journey forward. It shines a light on improving harmony in your world, and this is a blessing that has you feeling grateful.

June

9 Friday

You enter a time that brims with excitement as a whirlwind of activity enter your social life. It brings new energy that promotes interpersonal bonds. A refreshing change of pace draws invitations to mingle. It enables you to carve out time with friends and valued companions. It emphasizes engaging with your social life and sharing trailblazing discussions that light up growth pathways.

10 Saturday ~ Last Quarter Moon in Pisces 19:31

The changes ahead bring a new growth cycle into your life. If you have felt adrift lately, you can ground your energy in a unique journey forward. Information arrives that hits a sweet note in your life. Something important appears to bring rising prospects that expand the borders of your world. It draws an engaging and active time that nurtures thoughtful discussions with kindred spirits. As the wheel of fortune turns in your favor, you see a positive impact in your life.

11 Sunday ~ Mercury ingress Gemini 10:24, Mercury trine Pluto 10:27, Pluto ingress Capricorn 13:12, Venus square Jupiter 15:39

Today's Venus square Jupiter planetary alignment offers good things for your social life. It is the perfect time to engage with friends; lively discussions nurture creativity. It is a prime time for letting your hair down and having fun in a relaxing environment that draws stability into your world. It brings happy developments as life moves forward towards advancing your fortune forward.

JUNE

12 Monday

Life expands most gloriously as the path ahead clears. It brings a succession of possibilities that have you thinking about the future with a strategic focus. It draws an empowering chapter that creates fertile ground for your ideas and inspiration. New ideas inspire a time of growth, and this sees optimism surging. It offers room to grow your talents and extend your reach into a new area.

13 Tuesday

Curious events on the horizon bring an enterprising chapter to light. You unearth a fantastic journey that grows your abilities. Some streamlining and rearranging may be necessary to reveal the potential possible fully. It links you to exciting developments that grow your talents and advance your skills to the next level. It draws a prosperous time to work with your abilities and explore side pathways that encourage growth and learning.

14 Wednesday ~ Flag Day

Good fortune flows into your world and adds a dash of excitement. It has you dreaming big about the possibilities. It offers a spontaneous time of mingling with friends, and this social engagement brings a welcome sense of rejuvenation. A fresh cycle beckons your life as sharing with kindred spirits stirs the pot of possibilities. Being open to expanding your world helps you manifest pleasing results.

15 Thursday

News arrives that hits the sweet spot. It brings a lighter chapter that draws abundance and excitement into your world. New options pave the way forward for progress to occur. You reveal an avenue that offers growth, productivity, and expansion. It lets you dive into developing an area that provides room to expand horizons and heighten your career potential. A side trail soon blossoms.

June

16 Friday

You enter a cycle of increasing opportunity that enables growth to occur. Marking out the stepping stones helps you plot a course towards your dreams. Staying true to your spirit draws the correct situation into your life. It signifies a lucky chapter ahead associated with expansion. It brings life-changing possibilities that spark essential changes. It magically enriches your life as it brings the gift of happiness and abundance.

17 Saturday ~ Saturn turns Retrograde in Pisces 16:52

Saturn is a planet that rules boundaries, structure, and discipline. This retrograde draws fair and reasonable choices. Your decisions connect with karma to achieve a fair and beneficial outcome. Honesty, integrity, and impartial judgment are essential in making the right choices for your life. Facing the truth of a situation shines a light on where the scales may be tipped unevenly to one side, creating a sense of imbalance in your life.

18 Sunday ~ New Moon in Cancer 4:38, Father's Day (US)

The New Moon brings change into your life. You enter refreshing territory that draws an impressive time of developing goals. It lets you make strides towards improving your circumstances. New possibilities spring to life, drawing an enchanting chapter of magic and mayhem. It offers a refreshing social aspect; it connects you with opportunities to mingle and network with your broader social circle.

JUNE

19 Monday ~ Sun square Neptune 3:53, Jupiter sextile Saturn 15:53

Today, the Neptune square Sun aspect can water down your ambitions, leaving you feeling foggy and indecisive. If your vision feels clouded, going back over your plans can help make sure they continue to align with your vision for future growth. Recommitting to developing your career goals can help shift some of the clouds that hang over your working life today. If the boss gives you a hard time, blame it on Neptune for bringing Monday woes into your working life.

20 Tuesday

You are ready for change and dive into a transition that will carry you forward toward new possibilities. You have been through a challenging chapter but can soon lift the lid on new options that inspire growth in your life. An emphasis on improving your situation draws a pleasing result. Several cross-currents flow into your life; listening to your intuition will give you a clear direction to develop your goals moving forward.

21 Wednesday ~ Midsummer/Litha Solstice 14:58, Mercury sextile Mars 15:23

The Mercury sextile Mars aspect today fosters joint projects and cooperation. Getting involved with a group endeavor stimulates your mind and brings new possibilities. Brainstorming sessions offer a trailblazing path towards innovative solutions and rising prospects. Joining forces and strategizing with like-minded people cultivate an excellent success rate. It helps you cover the bases by blending other people's talents into the mix of potential at your disposal.

22 Thursday

The twists and turns ahead keep you on your toes. It highlights surprise news arriving in your social life. It clears the way forward and lets you harness a sense of wanderlust and adventure. It draws an active and happy chapter of networking with friends and colleagues. You invest your time in a rewarding area that enriches your life. It takes you on a journey that captures the essence of excitement.

JUNE

23 Friday

Improving your circumstances is a consistent theme that hums along in the background of your life. It sweetens your journey by bringing new options to light that have you feeling excited about the potential possible. An active socializing time provides the perfect backdrop for stepping out in a community setting. It hits the ticket for a chapter that draws happiness and harmony into your surroundings.

24 Saturday

Connecting with your tribe brings new ideas and inspiration to the forefront of your life. It blossoms into an enchanting journey that nurtures well-being and harmony. Nurturing your dreams soon brings a stunning viewpoint into view. News arrives that provides new information and insight into your social life. It does take you on a journey of happiness that advances life towards new projects.

25 Sunday

Life holds glittering options which encourage expansion. It advances you towards a progressive and prosperous journey that offers positive outcomes. It ushers in an expressive aspect that fosters growth in your social life. It launches a time of new projects and endeavors that open the door to rising prospects in your life. A productive and engaging time ahead fosters grounded foundations and sees well-being soaring.

JUNE

26 Monday ~ First Quarter Moon in Libra 7:50, Mars square Uranus 9:22

Good news arrives with a flurry of excitement. It helps you break free of limitations and focus on developing your goals. With the wind beneath your wings, you turn the corner and enjoy creating a new venture that catches your eye. Life brings an energetic and productive environment that expands the borders of your world. It lets you set sail on a timely voyage that boosts your abilities and develops your talents.

27 Tuesday ~ Mercury ingress Cancer 12:22

Creating space to nurture your talents draws an optimistic shift that carries you forward on a journey that marks a significant turning point in your life. It translates to new energy that encourages the continuation of a theme representing transformation. Riding a wave of good power opens the floodgates to new possibilities. A unique path calls your name, as expanding horizons offers a light aspect that draws fruitful results.

28 Wednesday

Favorable changes are coming up in your life. It helps you push back the barriers that limit progress and create a bridge to a brighter future. A landmark opportunity emerges to inspire expansion in your life. It brings a path that reveals a prominent area worth investigating. Focusing on developing your dreams brings a worthwhile mission. It gives you free rein to expand creatively into new regions.

29 Thursday ~ Sun trine Saturn 1:42

Today's Sun trine Saturn offers constructive dialogues and thoughtful ideas that enhance your creativity and stimulate new pathways of possibility in your life. A positive influence nurtures unique approaches that capitalize on the potential possible in your surroundings. You pass the threshold and enter a brighter, happier time of progressing goals. It gets a boost that lifts flagging spirits. It brings a connected time that offers a wellspring of support.

J̲U̲L̲Y̲

Sun	Mon	Tue	Wed	Thu	Fri	Sat
						1
2	3	4	5	6	7	8
9	10	11	12	13	14	15
16	17	18	19	20	21	22
23	24	25	26	27	28	29
30	31					

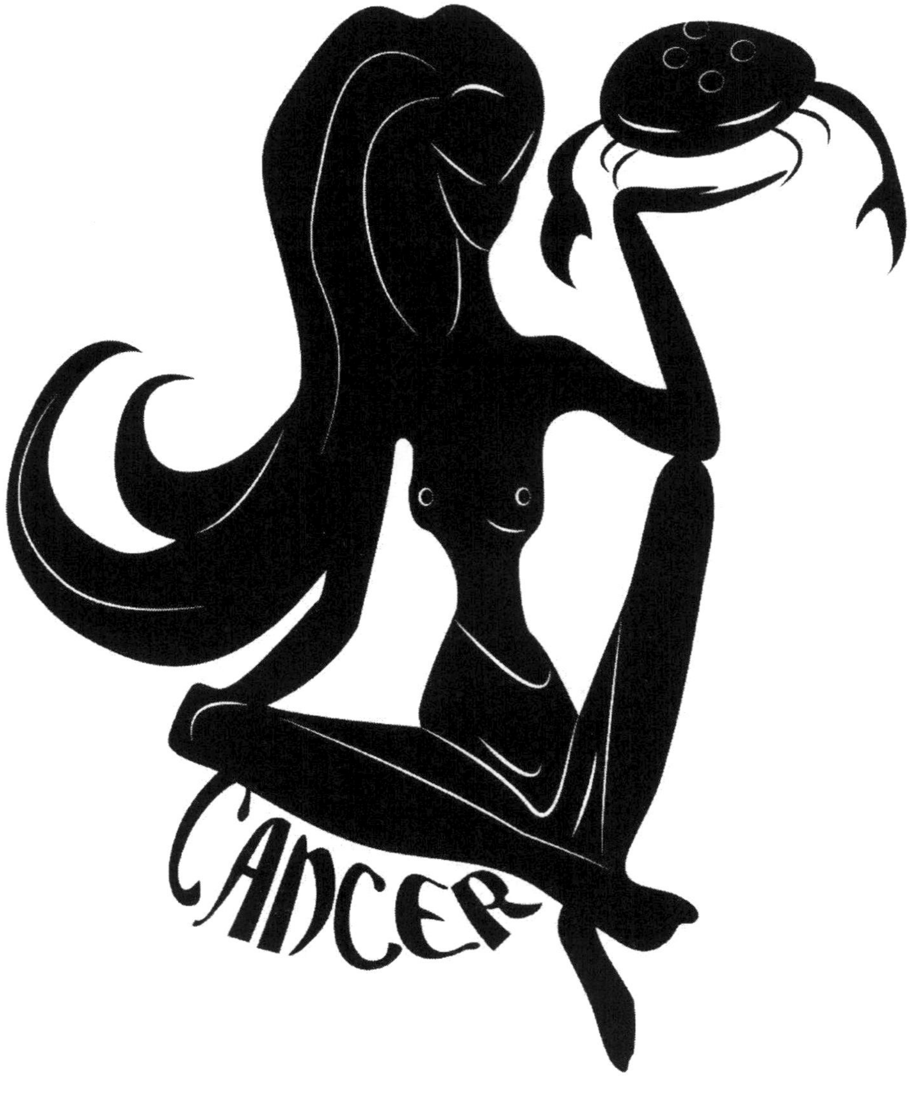
CANCER

New Moon

Buck Moon

June/July

30 Friday ~ Neptune turns Retrograde in Pisces, 19:28

Neptune retrograde strips away delusions, allusions, and fanciful thinking. Under the glare of more informed thought processes, you build tangible growth pathways to take your talents to the next level. This phase enables you to sink your teeth into developing goals that offer fruitful results. Moving away from areas that have clouded your thinking and brought doubt to your judgment does provide you with clear stepping stones that take you towards success.

1 Saturday ~ Canada Day, Sun conjunct Mercury 5:05, Mercury sextile Jupiter 7:10, Sun sextile Jupiter 10:26

Open-mindedness, curiosity, and a quest for adventure are prominent aspects as a Mercury sextile Jupiter alignment fosters creativity and self-expression. This transit favors organization, planning, and the development of longer-term goals. Reviewing plans and streamlining your vision enables you to cut to the chase and find a practical path to progress your goals. New information emerges to catch your interest and spur you to advance your life.

2 Sunday ~ Venus square Uranus 14:32

An increased need for freedom and liberation can destabilize as Venus faces Uranus in a square alignment. Being mindful of balancing interpersonal bonds while being self-expressive and creative can ease tensions. At the same time, you can let your hair down and enjoy a freedom-driven chapter of fun and excitement. It begins a fantastic voyage that offers room to progress your life as you mindfully head towards smoother sailing.

July

3 Monday ~ Super Moon, Buck Full Moon in Capricorn 11:40

The Full Moon brings new potential flowing into your life. It offers a path that nurtures your soul with new possibilities. Being mindful of the blessings that seek to enter your world draws abundance in your life. It brings an ambient environment that lets you step back and gain a broader perspective on the path ahead. It offers a shift towards a harmonious time of self-development.

4 Tuesday ~ Independence Day

A new journey ahead lets you engage with expanding the borders of your world. It launches a social time that lightens life as it draws well-being and happiness into your world. It brings a happy chapter that rules expansion as you get busy engaging with your social life. It brings a bustling time of heading out and about with friends. Invitations to mingle soon crop up in your life.

5 Wednesday

Being open to new people and experiences draws a bonus into your social life. You connect with a companion who offers thoughtful discussions and supportive energy. A gateway onward brings a journey of excitement and adventure. It emphasizes improving your foundations and enhancing the stability possible in your world. It brings the opportunity to socialize with friends and mingle in your broader community environment.

6 Thursday

The changes ahead bring a positive aspect into your life. Reward and happiness run rife as new ideas and epiphanies set in motion the development of unique adventures that inspire growth. You take a journey encompassing your dreams and desires as you grow your goals, talents, and skills. You shape your life as you see fit. Making yourself a priority brings good luck and prosperity into your world.

July

7 Friday

It marks a time that rules expansion in your life. A positive influence ahead helps you nurture a bond that holds room to grow into a meaningful path forward in your life. It is the continuation of a more comprehensive theme of change and discovery that currently surrounds your life. It brings an enriching time that offers lively discussions and thoughtful ideas. It opens the gate to new possibilities.

8 Saturday

News makes an entrance that brings a flurry of excitement into your life. It draws an engaging and lively environment that sets the stage for growth in your world. An emphasis on building solid foundations promotes harmony. A positive influence helps you craft your vision and develop a dream aspect for your life. You open a new chapter and discover a vast landscape of possibility tempting you forward.

9 Sunday ~ Mercury trine Neptune 23:56

Mercury in trine with Neptune focuses on your dreams and goals; it adds mental clarity that helps you stay focused as you work towards realizing your vision. Something you hope to reach in your life can reach fruition with the correct planning, adjustments, and focus. Creating space to nurture your priorities lets you reap the rewards of a dedicated approach that offers an increasing success rate.

July

10 Monday ~ Last Quarter Moon in Aries 1:48, Mars ingress Virgo 11:34, Mercury opposed Pluto 20:47

Today encourages you to expand your horizons into new areas. It means stepping out of your comfort zone and developing regions that come calling to grow your talents. Rising creativity and adaptability help you seize opportunities that come your way. Learning and growth are at the crux of an extended time of reaching for your dreams. News arrives, which brings a boost.

11 Tuesday ~ Mercury ingress Leo 4:09

Improvement ahead boosts your confidence and brings lighter energy into your life. It helps you harness creative abilities and develop your skills as you head towards rising possibilities in your life. It takes you towards a prosperous landscape that offers advancement as you gain traction on growing your world. It provides a productive time that nurtures growth and stability.

12 Wednesday

Being open to new possibilities draws a pleasing result. News arrives that has you feeling excited about prospects. It helps you take steps towards developing a long-held dream. You become busy in an engaging and dynamic environment that kickstarts a journey toward growth. It brings the perfect time for cooking up a storm of new ideas. It helps with progressing goals forward. Planning is instrumental in making the most of opportunities that cross your path.

13 Thursday

There may be an influence holding you back from reaching for your dreams. Taking a moment to release any areas that limit progress helps you build stable foundations. You soon realize that things are ready to shift forward in your life. You won't have to wait long as news arrives, bringing new information to your door. It attracts something you have been seeking into your life. It opens to a time that offers many blessings as you progress towards rising prospects.

July

14 Friday ~ Sun sextile Uranus 23:02

In sextile with the Sun, Uranus captures the essence of surprises, new information, and discoveries. Something new and exciting is ready to manifest in your life. Being open to new people and possibilities charts a course towards rising prospects. A joyous time ahead highlights improvement flowing into your world. It emphasizes developing bonds that offer room to grow your social life.

15 Saturday

Exploring new options draws a fresh wind into your life. It carries lighter energy that helps you create space to move in alignment with events that tempt you forward. It brings social opportunities to connect with others, which offers an emotionally happy time. It paves the way for a lively environment of entertaining and sharing with friends. Dreams take flight under sunny skies, bringing laughter and liveliness into your life.

16 Sunday

Keeping the bar raised does offer long-term benefits. It helps you sift and sort the path ahead and move away from areas that fail to reach fruition. A whirlwind of activity overhead draws new options into your life. It ushers in an essential phase of expanding horizons and active involvement with your broader social life. Life blossoms with opportunities to mingle, and you soon build stable foundations in your home life.

July

17 Monday ~ Mercury square Jupiter 12:48, New Moon in Cancer 18:32

You gently set the essence of manifestation in motion, which propels you towards developing new goals. It marks the beginning of a productive phase, a ticket for growth, leading to rising prospects. Progressing your plans forward helps ground your energy in a journey that cultivates well-being and harmony. Sharing with friends tones down stress levels and nurtures your environment with fruitful possibilities.

18 Tuesday ~ Islamic New Year

The tides turn in your favor as a positive influence brings exciting prospects to the surface. It brings expansion that enables you to fill depleted emotional tanks with engaging conversations and a heightened sense of well-being. It lays the foundations for a stable and balanced journey. Working with your creative abilities has a profound effect on improving your circumstances.

19 Wednesday

Something new and exciting emerges to tempt you forward. Your eye for detail spots a fantastic opportunity ahead that offers wide-ranging benefits. It expands your social life and connects you with companions who offer thoughtful discussions around unique areas. It brings a creative element as you head towards change and try your hand at something new.

20 Thursday ~ Sun trine Neptune 13:06, Mars opposed Saturn 20:39

The Sun trine Neptune alignment raises the vibration around your life. It focuses on improving the circumstances in your life and helping others who face difficult circumstances. Creativity is a valuable resource that lets you craft plans that offer tangible impacts that enhance your world. Positive news arrives soon. It shines a light on what is possible when thinking outside the box. It does bring a mood boost that draws beneficial options into your life.

July

21 Friday

Life heads to an upswing as you find solutions and head toward growth. Finding your balance in an ever-changing environment makes you discover learning and progression pathways. Bright and cheerful energy flows into your life, harmonizing and balancing your spirit. Possibilities ahead fascinate and mesmerize as you contemplate the path forward with an eye for detail. It opens to a busy time that lets you embrace growing your life.

22 Saturday ~ Sun opposed Pluto 3:52

The Sun shines a light on a hidden aspect Pluto keeps out of sight in your day-to-day life. This opposition Pluto creates a doorway through which pockets of the inner self, spirit, and primal energy can reach the surface of your awareness. It shines a light on subconscious desires and instincts. Life has an edgier aspect that can feel unsettling today. It does get you in touch with hidden depths that spark an internal dialogue as you reveal a personal element of your personality.

23 Sunday ~ Venus turns Retrograde in Leo 1:33, Sun ingress Leo 1:47

Venus turns retrograde, which slows the progress down around your love life. Romantic development slows down or stagnates during this phase. Focus on the building blocks as the journey is as important as the final destination. You can set boundaries with areas that leave you feeling drained. Conserving your emotional energy leaves you feeling more empowered and ready to tackle new projects and endeavors.

JULY

24 Monday

News arrives that brings a lucky break. This surprise emerges out of the blue and fills your life with excitement. It helps you make the most of growing your world outwardly. Being open to new opportunities ahead lights up your life with possibility and potential. An incoming assignment sparks a busy time that brings glorious developments around creativity and expression. You continue to branch out and create forward momentum to improve your bottom line.

25 Tuesday ~ First Quarter Moon in Libra 22:06

Life stirs up exciting endeavors that spark growth in your world. It brings an ambitious project that helps you unleash your talents on a path that offers rising prosperity. In this lush and rich landscape, you grow your abilities and head towards advancement. Nurturing your skills feeds creativity and heightens the potential possible in your life. As the tone shifts and lighter, enthusiasm weaves gently around your circumstance.

26 Wednesday

Listen to your instincts and pay attention to clues as they arrive. Opportunity comes knocking and brings new potential into your life, removing the heaviness. As you focus on developing unique options, you gain insight into other dreams and aspirations. A time of adventure ahead fuels your imagination with creative inspiration. It lets you pass the threshold and cross over to a lighter and happier landscape.

27 Thursday ~ Mercury conjunct Venus 15:15

The Mercury conjunct Venus aspect today bodes well for your personal life. Communication flows, as does feelings, emotions, and sentiments. The time is right to share loving thoughts and receive positive feedback from someone who holds meaning in your life. It helps build a stable foundation that sees improvement flowing into your life. A social aspect restores equilibrium; it gives you a rock-solid foundation to expand your life.

July

28 Friday ~ Delta Aquarids Meteor Shower. July 12th – August 23rd, Mercury ingress Virgo 21:29

You are headed towards change as your situation is currently evolving. Being open to new possibilities uncovers pathways that take you towards growth. It brings a passageway towards a brighter future. It helps you step out into an environment filled with blossoming activity ahead. You unwrap a time of endless possibilities, engaging activities, and expansion.

29 Saturday

Adjusting to new circumstances is never easy but creating a stable foundation enables you to move forward in a balanced manner. It brings sound energy that sees life evolving and becoming more prosperous. It positions you to develop a journey that nurtures an abundant landscape as you touch down on a new chapter of possibility for your life. You can cast your net wide and discover new leads.

30 Sunday

It rules a time of expansion that helps you extend your reach and promote a new growth area. It draws an emotionally balanced and stable foundation into your home life. It brings a rising aspect to the realms of your emotions, creativity, and intuition. It helps you weather challenges and draws emotional stability into your world. You steer clear of drama, choosing a balanced and calm approach to life.

August

Sun	Mon	Tue	Wed	Thu	Fri	Sat
		1	2	3	4	5
6	7	8	9	10	11	12
13	14	15	16	17	18	19
20	21	22	23	24	25	26
27	28	29	30	31		

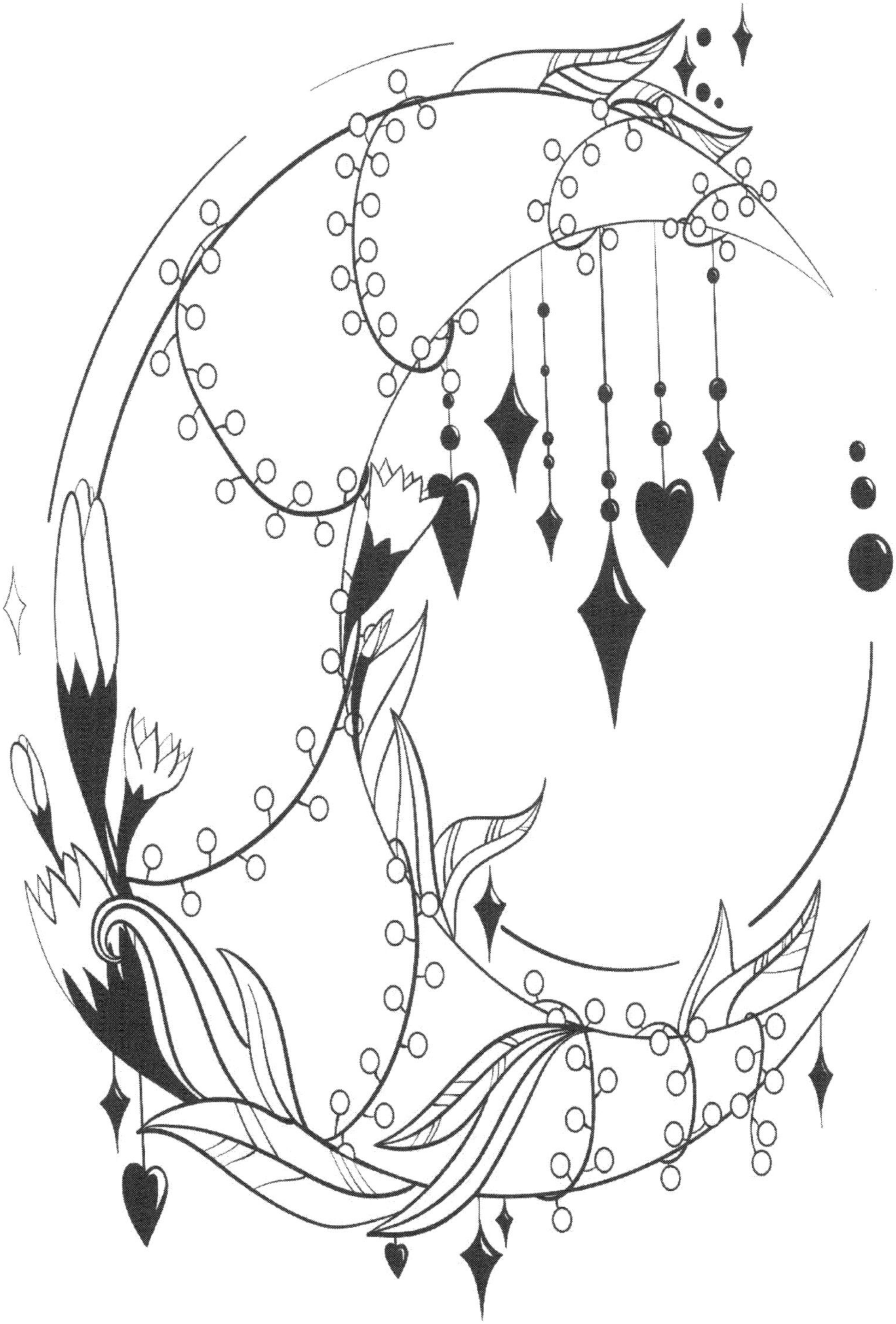

New Moon

Sturgeon Moon

July/August

31 Monday

Prospects are rising, and this breathes new life into your dreams. Clearing blocks and establishing stable foundations lights a path of growth around your life. You discover unique areas that encourage expansion. Sifting and sorting ideas helps you refine and blend the potential into a unique approach. Further options to spark your interest, marking a turning point that lets you head towards growth and prosperity.

1 Tuesday ~ Lammas/Lughnasadh, Super Moon, Sturgeon Full Moon in Aquarius 18:32, Mars trine Jupiter 20:44

The Full Moon offers a time of thoughtful discussions that draw rejuvenation. You land in an enriching environment that removes the heaviness as you head towards growth. It provides a bright and optimistic journey towards nurturing your dreams. Making yourself a priority creates space to promote peace in your surroundings. Setting boundaries with toxic areas serves your spirit well.

2 Wednesday ~ Mercury opposed Saturn 2:16

As Mercury opposes Saturn, it brings heavy vibes into your life. The air of tension leaves a palpable sense of negativity around conversations and communication today. A serious-minded person may seek to have a strongly worded conversation with you. Setting boundaries and creating space to nurture the foundations in your life helps restore balance if talks become pessimistic today. Pushing business decisions off for another day is advisable.

3 Thursday

There is a lot of growth ahead in your life. Priorities shift and change as you become aware of the heightened opportunities ahead that promote an active skill development phase. Refining your talents brings a time that sees you working with your creativity and progressing your abilities. It cranks up the potential possible in your world and offers to extend your reach into a new area.

August

4 Friday

Inspiration flows into your life and brings with it the winds of change. A creative idea takes shape; you have the talents needed to make this venture a reality. Indeed, nurturing your inspiration and working with your abilities grounds your energy in an enterprising environment. It draws kindred spirits into your life who share your passion for life. New options crop up that help you forge ahead and try your luck in a new area.

5 Saturday

News arrives that brings a bright flavor to your life. It removes nervous and outworn energy. Releasing areas that are no longer relevant helps you forge a secure foundation. It is instrumental in discovering a new possibility that flings open the door to a journey that grows your situation. Under the influence of positive news, you advance your life and transition forward to a new chapter of potential.

6 Sunday

You crack open a chapter that encourages growth and lets you move towards achieving your goals. As you advance in alignment with your soul direction, you look toward others for wisdom and guidance. Your potential moves forward in leaps and bounds as you embrace a journey that speaks to your heart. Creativity heightens, bringing new endeavors to explore. It brings the perfect environment for growing your talents and advancing onward.

August

7 Monday ~ Sun square Jupiter 12:03

Today's Sun square Jupiter aspect raises confidence and brings good fortune swirling around your life. It does boost your ego, which could lead to you overstepping the mark. Knowing your capabilities and working within the systems you have in place for your life will help keep things in check during this energetic time. Consistency and balance draw grounded foundations that help you move sustainably towards progression.

8 Tuesday ~ Last Quarter Moon in Taurus 10:48

You stand on the precipice of change and progression. News arrives that sets your life ablaze with remarkable possibilities. It propels you towards a journey of promise and excitement. It brings a shift forward that offers a lovely boost to highlight new options worth developing. It encourages expansion and lets you create abundance by exploring all that life offers during this time.

9 Wednesday ~ Venus square Uranus 11:09

A surprise element adds a sense of uncertainty to your personal/social life due to the Venus square Uranus aspect today. It positions you to improve your social life and direct your energy into achieving a fantastic result. Adventure comes calling and lets you chart a course towards a boatload of golden options. New potential arrives in waves bringing news and information that sparks a transition forward. It is an inspiring time that shines a light on nurturing your dreams.

10 Thursday ~ Mercury at Greatest Elongation 27.4 E, Mercury trine Jupiter 12:45

Mercury trine Jupiter today brings a boost into your life. Jupiter is the planet of good luck and fortuitous happenings, which improves the potential possible around your circumstances. A shift forward brings expansion. It offers positive change that lets you set your sights on a curious new enterprise. It draws abundance to your foundations, and this grounded energy creates a firm basis for growing your life.

August

11 Friday

Capturing the essence of efficiency, you operate effectively in a productive environment. It lets you create magic from your creativity and takes you toward an enchanting chapter of growing your vision. You discover several opportunities are swirling around your social life, tempting you towards sharing thoughts with others. It brings a lively environment that offers activities and sharing with friends.

12 Saturday ~ Perseids Meteor Shower July 17th - Aug 24th

Surprise news arrives that offers a promising sign which paves the way forward toward an area of growth. The light enters your life, bringing new exploration possibilities that complement your abilities. Extending the reach of your social circle helps you form a network of support. It brings kindred spirits together and leads to a chance to collaborate with another talented individual.

13 Sunday

News arrives that enables you to grow your vision. It brings insight into pathways that take your talents to the next level. It brings an excellent outlet for excess energy and uses your creativity to advance your situation. Making the most of your skillset draws a pleasing outcome. It reveals a positive aspect that helps you thrive. Being open to new possibilities draws luck, people, and good fortune into your world. It

AUGUST

14 Monday

Unique opportunities are incoming which bring magic into your world. It offers a pivotal time for rising prospects that draw new possibilities into your life. It lets you set up growth as you spot an area for development that holds water. It highlights growth and expansion in your life that kicks off a positive trend. Working with your creativity magnifies the potential possible as you transition forward towards a fresh start.

15 Tuesday

New opportunities unlock the right path. It brings a sense of rejuvenation, giving you time to nurture your dreams. If you have been feeling adrift, you can use your abilities to bring goodness to the surface of your world. Being open to growing your life transitions you towards heightened opportunities. It shifts your mindset towards an abundant focus which improves your circumstances. An emphasis on enhancing foundations sees events move favorably.

16 Wednesday ~ Sun square Uranus 2:34, New Moon in Leo 09:37, Mars trine Uranus 13:53

Uranus steals the show today, and you can expect a spontaneous and expressive environment that offers a breath of fresh air in your life. Movement and discovery overhead brings a time of celebration that provides the chance to mingle and network with others. You soon break fresh ground and create space for something new to blossom. News arrives that draws sparks of excitement.

17 Thursday

Information arrives for you soon, which sparks your attention. Indeed, you are wise to stay open to new possibilities as this adds spice and flavor to your world. It triggers a social aspect that brings bright and cheerful energy your way. Sharing lively and entertaining conversations gets a boost that paves the way forward towards expanding horizons. You attract the right opportunities into your world.

August

18 Friday

You hit upon a new trend that brings positive opportunities into your world. It draws communication and messages. Information ahead lets you plot a course towards improving your social life. Change surrounds your world as an avenue opens that brings an exciting influence into your life. A spur-of-the-moment invitation brings excitement and adventure. It brings entertaining conversations and a lively atmosphere.

19 Saturday

News arrives that sees your fortune changing for the better. The currency of change surrounds you to tempt you towards growth. It offers new possibilities that ramp up potential. It brings the first step towards gaining solid growth, ensuring a stable shift towards developing your vision. It brings the sunshine and tells of blessings and promises fulfilled. It connects you with a social aspect that links you with kindred spirits.

20 Sunday

A time of blossoming creativity is looming that begins a new journey filled with hope and promise. Information arrives that encourages your continual evolution on this path of growth. You can cast your net wide and discover a fascinating area that inspires your mind. It has you dreaming big about future possibilities.

AUGUST

21 Monday

Improvement is coming into your world that lights up your life with new possibilities. It brings growth and prosperity that offers the gift of stability and long-term security. It draws a busy and active time of creating steady improvement. You are moving towards a new area that provides room to progress your talents. Planning a blueprint is instrumental in navigating the path ahead.

22 Tuesday ~ Venus square Jupiter 12:13, Mars opposed Neptune 20:33

A Venus Jupiter square offers rising prospects for your love life. You will have trouble concentrating on the task as fun moments capture your attention. An emphasis on improving your romantic life creates the right environment to see your personal life become more prosperous and more meaningful. It brings an upbeat time that offers a positive influence on your life. Troubles fade under sunny skies shared with a lively companion.

23 Wednesday ~ Sun ingress Virgo 8:58, Mercury turns retrograde 19:59

Mercury turns retrograde and puts a damper on the potential possible in your social life. It can cause miscommunication and issues in your love life. Mercury in retrograde adds an element that turns communication haywire. It disrupts the positive flow of energy in your life. Delay signing contracts or committing to business deals during a retrograde phase. It is an appropriate time for planning to launch new endeavors after the retrograde cycle.

24 Thursday ~ First Quarter Moon in Sagittarius 9:57

An opportunity arrives which resonates positively with your future goals. It lights you up with an area where you can grow your abilities and nurture your talents. It rules advancing life forward towards new endeavors. You plan and use strategy to reveal a prominent aspect that calls your name. It lets you achieve an active phase of progressing goals forward. Expanding your life has you focusing on an area that captures the essence of inspiration.

AUGUST

25 Friday ~ Mars trine Pluto 12:22

Today's aspect offers rising prospects for your career. It brings a goal-orientated, disciplined, and centered focus on improving your working life. New possibilities tempt you towards growth and expansion. Indeed, examining your goals brings further information that opens the way forward. A piece of your puzzle falls into place, bringing options that let you nail goals. It sets in motion an essence of manifestation that shifts your focus towards a long-term vision.

26 Saturday

Your life is transforming towards greener pastures. New possibilities ahead help create a stable platform from which to grow your life. Fresh ideas help you reveal a landscape of new opportunities. Life is ripening with refreshing options ready to bloom. It brings new goals to work towards as you get busy improving your circumstances. News arrives, which brings a boost to your spirit.

27 Sunday ~ Sun opposed Saturn 8:28, Mars ingress Libra r 13:15

Once you've had a chance to rest and catch your breath, you can use the downtime to improve foundations and release outworn areas that limit progress. Regular time away in your sanctuary brings a chance to think about the future and plot a course towards a venture that inspires your mind. It gets a lead that lets you open your world to new areas. Crunching the numbers allows you to do due diligence before embarking on a course of action.

AUGUST

28 Monday

A change ahead brings a turning point. It links you with a social environment that adds an exciting flavor to your life. Mingling and networking bring positive communication and conversations that see ideas flowing as possibilities abound. Life lightens, bringing laughter and renewal to your door. Expanding your horizons brings you in contact with inspiring people who nurture happiness in your life.

29 Tuesday ~ Uranus turns Retrograde in Taurus 2:11

Uranus moving into a retrograde phase boosts idealism; it offers big sky pictures that help motivate change to improve the world around you. This planetary cycle will boost your confidence and foster leadership qualities. It deepens initiative and offers a fresh wind that spurs creativity and an uptick of potential. It is the beginning of a new chapter that draws insight and inspiration as new goals flow freely, creating pathways of possibility.

30 Wednesday

The path ahead clears, seeing improvement flowing into your social life. It lets you take essential steps that advance your situation. Expanding horizons considers a new approach to taking prominence. It clears the air with your friends and brings improvements by increments to your broader social life. It brings a brighter outlook as a new energy flow draws vitality into your surroundings.

31 Thursday ~ Super Moon, Blue Full Moon in Pisces 1:36

The more you grow your spiritual path, the more you learn to connect with abundance. An area you become involved with developing draws a sense of changes into your world. Learning and growth spark a fresh start that evolves your abilities and expands your life. It sees you set your sights on a lofty goal that gives you the chance to grow your world. It leads to a significant time of discovery and expansion in your life.

SEPTEMBER

Sun	Mon	Tue	Wed	Thu	Fri	Sat
					1	2
3	4	5	6	7	8	9
10	11	12	13	14	15	16
17	18	19	20	21	22	23
24	25	26	27	28	29	30

wild SOUL

New Moon

Corn/Harvest Moon

SEPTEMBER

1 Friday

A refreshing change of pace draws new possibilities into your social life. It helps you shut the door on a challenging chapter and reboots the potential possible in your world. An impromptu get-together with friends draws lively discussions. It brings a strong emphasis on improving the foundations in your life. You unpack a colorful chapter that brings new possibilities to light. A positive change on the horizon seals the deal on a refreshing landscape of opportunity.

2 Saturday

News arrives, which bestows blessings as it brings a time of good fortune into your social life. It has you mingling with new people and developing a support network that nurtures lively discussions and interpersonal bonds. It brings a uniquely uplifting aspect that offers a wellspring of benefits for your spirit. Sharing thoughts and ideas with others is a soothing balm that settles your restless energy.

3 Sunday

Contemplating the choices around your life helps you gain greater clarity which lets you achieve a breakthrough. It opens a gateway forward that fuels excitement and adventure. It brings the essence of manifestation, which helps you progress toward goals. You land in an enriching environment that enables you to develop your vision. You soon find that things take shape in a unique setting. It helps you uncover a lead that nurtures the theme of prosperity.

September

**4 Monday ~ Labor Day, Venus turns direct in Leo 1:19,
Mercury trine Jupiter 10:29, Jupiter turns Retrograde in Taurus 14:14**

Venus turns direct and brings an open road of potential into your love life. It helps you develop a path towards your dreams. It lets you forge ahead and take in the planning of lofty goals. A strong emphasis on improving your home environment cultivates fresh energy that breaks up stagnant patterns. It heightens the potential in your romantic life, bringing a boost into your world.

5 Tuesday

New options shine brightly overhead. Changes on the horizon help you spring open the doors to a unique chapter in your life. It has you feeling lighter and more optimistic about future possibilities. Beautiful changes arrive, which promote attractive options. It shines a light on a positive influence that adds fuel to your creativity. It charts an auspicious journey towards a lush landscape of new possibilities ahead.

6 Wednesday ~ Sun conjunct Mercury 11: 08, Last Quarter Moon in Gemini 22:21

Independent thinking and innovative ideas can be attributed to the Sun, Mercury conjunct today. Life holds a curious twist that draws change that leads to advancement. You navigate a path towards growing your abilities. It brings an impressive time of pushing back limitations to reach a chosen destination. Funneling your excess energy into working with your abilities draws a pleasing result. It unearths new options for your career path.

7 Thursday

Being receptive to change helps you make the most of an incoming opportunity meant for your life. It gives you a nudge in the right direction as you get a clear picture of what is possible when expanding your reach into new areas. It is a journey that offers transformation and growth as a strong emphasis on growing your life connects you with rising prospects ahead.

SEPTEMBER

8 Friday ~ Sun trine Jupiter 11:12

The Sun forms a trine with Jupiter, which increases good luck and fortune in your life. A positive influence nurtures beneficial outcomes. Expanding your life lets you uncover a little nugget of gold worth exploring. You set sail on a voyage that offers happiness and abundance. It emphasizes growth, advancement, and prosperity. Nurturing your environment lets you branch out and extend your talents into new areas.

9 Saturday

A shift ahead brings new companions into your life. It does see someone step forward and begin nurturing a friendship with you. Indeed, being open to meeting new people helps you tap into unique opportunities that let you make strides towards improving your social life. It brings the right environment to promote social engagement and share a supportive and lively time with friends.

10 Sunday

Today speaks of improvement around your home and family life. It leads to a productive chapter that nurtures balanced foundations. Your life moves from strength to strength as you find your groove in a more social environment. A busy time ahead brings a productive landscape into view, which offers a sense of progression and growth. It draws emotional wellness as you transition forward with a unique perspective and a happy outlook on life.

September

11 Monday

Today opens the gateway towards a fresh start that sees you expanding life outwardly. Designing your life is a strong focus ahead which draws abundance into your surroundings. It brings a grounded and secure foundation from which to develop your world in a unique direction. A positive influence brings a vibrant landscape of possibility to your life.

12 Tuesday

Exploring ways to improve your circumstances brings a journey worth your time. It gives you a chance to transform your world and achieve growth and rising prospects. You soon open pathways that nurture a wellspring of abundance in your world. Being open to change helps the cream rise to the top as information arrives that shines a light on new goals for your life. A positively charged environment offers a wellspring of possibility.

13 Wednesday

The changes ahead draw new options into your world. These unique options help you unpack an engaging chapter that offers growth and rising prospects. Happy news ahead keeps your social life humming along. You receive invitations to mingle, which provide a welcome distraction and heightened well-being and happiness. You discover a lot of new energy, which ushers in fresh possibilities for your life.

14 Thursday

An emphasis on constructive dialogues seals the deal for a happier chapter. You begin to see some feel-good energy flowing into your social life, which lets you close the door to past problems. You can turn the tides in your favor by taking the time to nurture grounded foundations. Deep inner reflection and self-discovery ahead grow your spirit in a unique direction. It lets you create inroads in progressing life forward.

September

15 Friday ~ Rosh Hashanah (begins at sunset), New Moon in Virgo 1:40, Mercury turns direct at 20:20

Mercury turns direct, and this improves communication and interpersonal bonds. It offers a renewed interest in your social life that helps harmonize frazzled tensions that occurred during the retrograde phase. Life takes on a lighter tone when exchanges with friends draw an active and engaging environment. A window of opportunity opens, bringing excitement ahead.

16 Saturday ~ Sun trine Uranus 1:23

The Sun trine Uranus aspect today adds a dash of spontaneity and excitement into your life. It is a favorable aspect that brings the freedom-driven chapter to light. Focusing on your social life draws a pleasing result as you connect with kindred spirits who offer excitement and passion. It helps set new goals, bringing your energy up a notch. It gets a chance for artistic expression and mingling with others who support your growth.

17 Sunday ~ Rosh Hashanah (ends at sunset), Venus square Jupiter 6:12

The Venus square Jupiter aspect makes it the perfect day for unwinding and relaxing with your social circle. An easy-going vibe draws thoughtful conversations and entertaining ideas. A chance to collaborate draws a valuable sense of kinship. Your intuition guides this journey; trust the process and keep expectations flexible. A focus on productivity lets you head towards your vision.

SEPTEMBER

18 Monday

News arrives that draws a busy and productive time. It brings ambitious ideas and helps you progress your reach into a new area. Working smarter draws a goal-orientated chapter that enables you to snag the next rung of the ladder in your career path. It marks a time of focusing on an enterprise that offers growth and prosperity. It brings luck and good fortune in the matters of your career aspect.

19 Tuesday ~ Sun opposed Neptune 11:17

Your perception broadens as the Sun lights up Neptune's dreamy aspects. Engaging with creativity and imagination draws rising ideas and innovative concepts to consider. Optimism is a golden key that opens the path to new possibilities. You soon establish your abilities in an area ripe for growth and build security in your world. A curious message crosses your path ahead, tempting you to explore a phase of increasing potential.

20 Wednesday

A creativity boost focuses on implementing new strategies and plans that increase the potential possible. It brings communication; it offers a chance to venture into a new area. Discipline and perseverance help you stick with the correct strategy that takes you towards success. Assertive energy in the air boosts confidence and high potential. A joint project or endeavor comes into focus and brings an enriching chapter ahead.

21 Thursday ~ International Day of Peace, Sun trine Pluto 5:20

Creating a strategy and working on the building blocks allows a solid foundation to emerge. It brings rising prospects, and as you begin growing your world, new options crop up to inspire change. You will appreciate the differences ahead as they closed the door on a problematic chapter. Being flexible and understanding helps you navigate a difficult time and reach a balanced environment that gives you more harmony and security. You settle into a lively atmosphere that generates well-being and happiness.

SEPTEMBER

22 Friday ~ Sun ingress Libra 6:46, First Quarter Moon in Sagittarius 19:32, Mercury at Greatest Elongation 17.9W

News ahead helps you settle into a grounded groove that offers a new approach to life. It focuses on rising well-being and happiness as you direct your attention towards areas that hold the most significant meaning in your life. A time of lively discussions brings a vibrant flavor into your life as the path ahead clears and you get busy with a time of expansion.

23 Saturday ~ Mabon/Fall Equinox 6:50

Information arrives that grows your life experience by opening some more meaningful goals. It culminates in a shift forward that offers advancement around your life. It attracts a rich landscape of potential that sees your creativity rising under sunny skies. A new realm of options draws a rewarding result. Rising prospects shine a light on new areas worth your time.

24 Sunday ~ Yom Kippur (begins at sunset)

There is a focus on self-development that nurtures well-being. It brings balance and stability into your home life. You make headway around finding a path forward that improves your circumstances. It creates a shift that blesses your life on many levels. Advancement is looming, which opens the floodgates toward growth and prosperity. It draws a lucrative and active chapter of expanding your life into new areas.

September

25 Monday ~ Yom Kippur (ends at sunset), Mercury trine Jupiter 12:12

Today's Mercury trine Jupiter aspect brings optimism and good news. Research, learning, study, and socializing are favored. This trine is ideal for formulating new plans and engaging in future-orientated brainstorming sessions. It's also the perfect time to sort and organize; your office, workspace, closet, or even your whole life. As creativity heightens, it pulls curious options to contemplate.

26 Tuesday

You score an assignment that captures the essence of creativity. It sees you bleeding with your imagination and heading towards an agreeable time of developing an area of interest in your life. Rising prospects soon bring transformation swelling into your world. It offers room to improve your bottom line and work on developing some nuggets of gold that help you migrate away from outworn areas. It ushers in change, discovery, and rejuvenation.

27 Wednesday

The path ahead sets all kinds of potential in motion for your life. It brings a bright passage forward towards developing unique goals. Your flexibility and creativity are valuable tools that help you chart a course toward growing your dreams. Nurturing the foundations in your life attracts a wellspring of possibilities. You soon direct your attention towards developing a goal that advances your talents.

28 Thursday

A new influence arrives in your life. It emphasizes reaching for your dreams and soon grounds your energy in a productive journey forward. Life becomes more accessible, expansive, and involved. It sees inspiration flowing into your world, restoring faith in the path ahead. It drives a social and comprehensive chapter of connecting with friends. News arrives that brings an invitation to mingle.

OCTOBER

Sun	Mon	Tue	Wed	Thu	Fri	Sat
1	2	3	4	5	6	7
8	9	10	11	12	13	14
15	16	17	18	19	20	21
22	23	24	25	26	27	28
29	30	31				

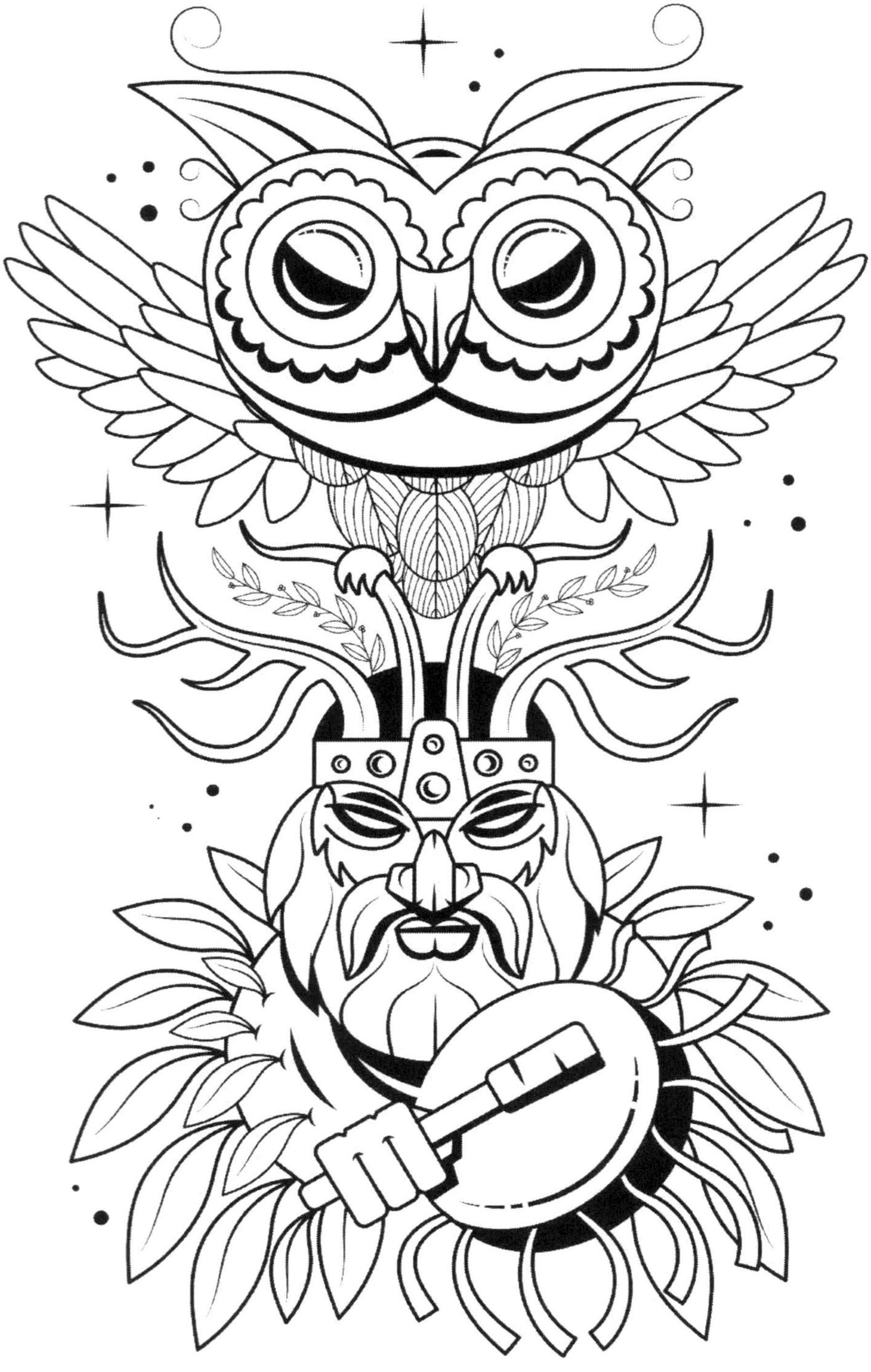

New Moon

Hunters Moon

September/October

29 Friday ~ Sukkot (begins at sunset), Super Moon, Corn Moon, Harvest Full Moon in Aries 9:58, Venus square Uranus 17:53

A restless vibe caused by a Venus Uranus square could undermine the security in your love life or the broader social environment if you are single. A freedom-loving vibration brings a need to be spontaneous and engage in unique adventures that change the day-to-day routine of your life. It sees progress occurring in your social life. It brings companionship and a sense of connection.

30 Saturday ~Mercury trine Uranus 16:56

Today's trine is perfect for using technology to keep life supported and flowing in your social life. Communication is your passageway to a more connected social life. Being innovative and thinking outside the box connects you with diverse pathways of growth and expansion. It brings a sense of fun and excitement into your social life. It offers lively sessions of sharing thoughts and ideas with someone who understands.

1 Sunday

A door opens, which brings communication into your world. It helps you embrace a more socially active environment. You are moving away from the stormy backdrop that has stalled progress for a while. Expanding the boundaries in your world sees a new friendship blossom into life. It brings lively discussions and an expansive chapter that feels right for your world. You soon channel your energy into developing an area that holds meaning.

OCTOBER

2 Monday ~ Mercury opposed Neptune 3:34

The Mercury and Neptune opposition helps you communicate your ideas and thoughts today. However, You may find work challenging as rising creativity brings a desire to daydream. Streamlining and refining your vision draws a flow of new possibilities. It puts you in the correct alignment to make the most of your talents. Cultivating your gifts unearths advancement that takes your abilities towards a lofty goal.

3 Tuesday ~ Mercury trine Pluto 19:20

New leads bring an influx of possibilities that opens the floodgates to an enterprising chapter. Creativity and confidence heighten, leaving you feeling encouraged to try learning new areas. Broadening your horizons lets you explore leads that offer room to grow and flourish. It marks an inspiring time that enables you to move ahead on a clearly defined mission. A venture you become involved with lights a path towards success.

4 Wednesday

A business idea takes off and blossoms into a venture worth developing. Soon enough, you see positive signs that feel encouraging. It focuses on expansion as it cracks the code to a well-designed journey that supports well-being and growth. It increases optimism and improves your life by letting you reshape goals and plot a course towards advancement. Wisely investing your time draws dividends.

5 Thursday ~ Mercury ingress Libra 12:06

Mercury can bring an indecisive vibe that causes stagnant energy. Procrastination can be an issue that delays progress in the workplace. Focusing on removing distractions and streamlining your environment can help mitigate the effect of this transit. Life moves from strength to strength as you become adept at navigating in a changing climate. Growing your talents brings an energizing time that offers advancement and success.

OCTOBER

6 Friday ~ Sukkot (ends at sunset), Last Quarter Moon in Cancer 13:48

News arrives that brings a burst of inspiration and opportunity. It breathes life into your surroundings and provides an avenue to grow your talents. Gifts of creativity that are currently dormant soon flourish under a prosperous sky. It drives the freedom-loving chapter that liberates your mood and offers an influx of options to tempt you towards growth. Manifestation gently flows through your life, bringing the correct path forward.

7 Saturday ~ Draconids Meteor Shower. Oct 6-10

Life brings opportunities that help in many ways. It lets you spread your wings and soar to great heights as a new adventure comes calling. It lights a path of valuable growth that enables you to maneuver forward and embrace developing your vision. A lovely perk arrives, which encourages a shift onward that has you exploring a journey that makes your heart sing. It turns your attention to a new chapter that draws abundance.

8 Sunday

It is the right time to create a vision board and put various options out there to contemplate. After a time of soul-searching, you touch down a path that highlights new possibilities—getting involved in advancing your abilities dials up your unique brand of wisdom and knowledge. It shines a light on advancing your abilities and extending your reach into new areas. It draws a busy time that offers news and information.

October

9 Monday ~ Thanksgiving Day (Canada), Indigenous People's Day, Columbus Day, Mars square Pluto 1:04, Venus ingress Virgo 1:06

There is plenty of support coming that brings good fortune, transformational experiences, and sudden news. It brings an active and dynamic environment that announces a fresh chapter. It improves your life as it gets a project that has you feeling inspired. You close a deal that offers valuable rewards. It does have you setting off on a new adventure, and this provides tips on many levels.

10 Tuesday ~ Venus opposed Saturn at 6:11. Pluto turns direct at 11:43

Being mindful of goals and dreams helps create a journey towards your vision. It brings a sense of purpose and added momentum into your life. It lets you move forward with courage and conviction as you open a new chapter in your book of life. It has you feeling optimistic about the potential possible in your world. It brings a time of planning, strategy, and investigation. Following your hunch enables you to unearth a lead that holds water.

11 Wednesday

A new possibility creates a stir of excitement. It reveals information that lets you plot a course towards developing a curious venture. It bestows blessing and opens your life to new pathways. A time of heightening creativity and expansion enables you to tackle an ambitious project. Life becomes busy, giving you the proper nourishment to spread your wings and map out new goals. You maintain stable foundations and draw security into your home life.

12 Thursday ~ Mars ingress Scorpio 3:59

News arrives soon, which brings a snap decision. Exciting changes sweep into your life and smooth out what has been a bumpy ride. It brings opportunities for growth that let you tackle an inspiring area. It brings a fertile environment from which to grow your life. Life picks up steam, opening your world to new flavors and possibilities. It draws security and provides the grounded platform in which to thrive.

October

13 Friday ~ Mars trine Saturn 12:28

The Mars trine Saturn aspect today boosts your working life. It enables you to gain traction on achieving a successful result. It puts the finishing touches on your working week as you meet deadlines with ease. This robust transit gives you the strength, ambition, and perseverance to take on the most complex tasks and complete them on time. Increased productivity and efficiency get the job done. Your self-discipline keeps you focused without being distracted or discouraged.

14 Saturday ~ New Moon in Libra 17:54, Annular Solar Eclipse 17:59

Intuitive choices bring new possibilities into your life. It provides an essential phase of expansion, growth, and opportunity. Getting involved in creating a life of your making helps smooth over the rough edges and lets you set sail towards smoother sailing. Taking action is a positive step that nurtures your life from the ground up. You discover strength, courage, and conviction that propels you forward to new challenges.

15 Sunday

Changes ahead draw a social environment that brings expansion. It lights a path glittering with new possibilities. It attracts new companions and offers an enriching chapter that illustrates the many blessings open in your world. There is a focus on security and establishing grounded foundations that bring balance and abundance into your world. A time of steady growth and development lets you accomplish a great deal and head towards new goals.

October

16 Monday

Keeping your eyes looking for new possibilities draws a pleasing result. It brings a promising lead that soon generates growth. It marks a time of significant change that hints at better days to come. It sharpens your skills, refines your abilities, and clearly understands the path ahead. Putting the pieces of this jigsaw together, you soon begin to see a broader picture of potential.

17 Tuesday

It speaks of a landmark time that offers new potential. It brings a floodlight of possibilities to see your perspective changing and evolving. It offers a path that grows your abilities and refines your talents. A brighter aspect lets you chart a course towards developing an area of interest. A decision ahead enables you to take advantage of a special offer; it brings a new role into focus.

18 Wednesday

A shift occurs that brings fundamental changes into your life. Information arrives that shines a light on a refreshing chapter. It opens the gate to a happy environment that connects you with your broader social circle. A focus on emotional wellness removes the drama and opens the floodgates to a vibrant time of new possibilities. It brings a chance to catch up with friends, which harmonizes foundations.

19 Thursday

A path ahead becomes a prominent aspect. It highlights social gatherings and a chance to mingle with friends. It brings a sense of connection, and harmony comes into focus as you blaze a path towards a refreshing destination. It aligns you with growth and security. It puts you in contact with others who offer guidance and support. It brings the horizon-broadening chapter that lifts your spirits and brings a boost to your world.

October

20 Friday ~ Sun conjunct Mercury 5:37

In conjunction with Mercury, the Sun is a favorable aspect that attracts communication. It is the best of all elements for receiving or sending communication. Interacting with others is vital today. It stimulates your need to share ideas and engage in thoughtful discussions that nurture well-being and harmony in your life. A moment of clarity brings a light bulb moment that offers curious insight into a new path forward. It brings change and progress ahead.

21 Saturday ~ Orionids Meteor Shower Oct 2nd – Nov 7th, Mercury square Pluto 12:50, Sun square Pluto 14:09

Today's aspect causes a challenging environment as you find your judgment or authority tested. Being challenged and put to the test feels uncomfortable as you think you are making the right choices and decisions for your life. The Mercury square Pluto transit also attracts interactions with other people who feed the gossip mill and cultivate drama, leading to a toxic environment.

22 Sunday ~ First Quarter Moon in Aquarius 03:29, Venus trine Jupiter 4:32, Mercury ingress Scorpio 6:46, Mercury trine Saturn 16:12

The Venus trine Jupiter aspect offers golden threads around your social and love life. It is one of the most anticipated transits which harmonizes interpersonal bonds and offers rising prospects of good luck to your romantic life. It is of particular interest to those seeking love or lovers wanting a deeper romantic bond.

OCTOBER

23 Monday ~ Venus at Greatest Elongation 46.4W, Sun ingress Scorpio 16:17

You enter a growth-orientated environment that lets you move forward in a stable and balanced fashion. It takes you towards great structure and stability in your life. It brings opportunities to advance your skills and evolve your talents. News arrives that delivers a boost as it places you in the proper alignment to extend your reach into a unique area that offers growth and rising prospects. It flings open the door to a sunny chapter ahead.

24 Tuesday ~ Sun trine Saturn 7:13

Today's Sun, Saturn trine, gives you a commanding presence in the workplace. Confidence peaks in mid-afternoon, enabling you to effectively manage the day's tasks with relative ease as your energy keeps humming along productively. You conquer the workload and achieve a robust result with your consistent and disciplined efforts, which draw a pleasing effect and the added benefits of increased job satisfaction.

25 Wednesday

focusing on improving your career path draws improvement. You enter a phase that sees growth and stability take shape. It advances your job prospects and sees you join a dynamic chapter ahead. Adjusting and refining your goals draws a productive chapter. You streamline your working life into an efficient powerhouse that lets you reach your goals with purpose. It helps create progress; information ahead brings insight into the blocks currently holding you back.

26 Thursday

Things are shifting towards change; life offers unique areas of growth and advancement. It brings new possibilities that help you advance towards your dreams. You open a book of chapters that connects with greater happiness in your life. It puts you in contact with like-minded people who celebrate your successes and share thoughtful discussions with you. Overall, the landscape ahead is expanding, encouraging progression.

October

27 Friday

A crossroads ahead brings two choices into your life. Information forward encourages you to walk a path in alignment with the person you are becoming. Transforming the potential flowing into your life builds better foundations that offer room to grow into a journey of wisdom and growth. It draws an environment that is soul-affirming and enriching. Lighter energy flows into your life with a gust of fresh air.

28 Saturday ~ Mars opposed Jupiter 16: 03, Hunters Full Moon in Taurus 20:23 Partial Lunar Eclipse 20:14

You can embrace one of the luckiest opposition aspects today when Mars opposes Jupiter and draws good fortune into your life. The winds of change carry news information into your surroundings. Today's transit increases your self-confidence and ability to handle your time and energy demands. It brings a competitive edge that fuels ambitions and the desire to achieve your goals.

29 Sunday ~ Mercury opposed Jupiter 3:44, Mercury conjunct Mars 14:21

Today, Mercury is the show's star and draws a favorable aspect that nurtures good fortune in your social life. It brings a chance to share with friends and loved ones. Relaxing and unwinding enable you to restore frazzled nerves and build robust foundations. It shines a light on an active time of mingling and socializing that draws abundance into your surroundings. Nurturing this area lights up new potential.

NOVEMBER

Sun	Mon	Tue	Wed	Thu	Fri	Sat
			1	2	3	4
5	6	7	8	9	10	11
12	13	14	15	16	17	18
19	20	21	22	23	24	25
26	27	28	29	30		

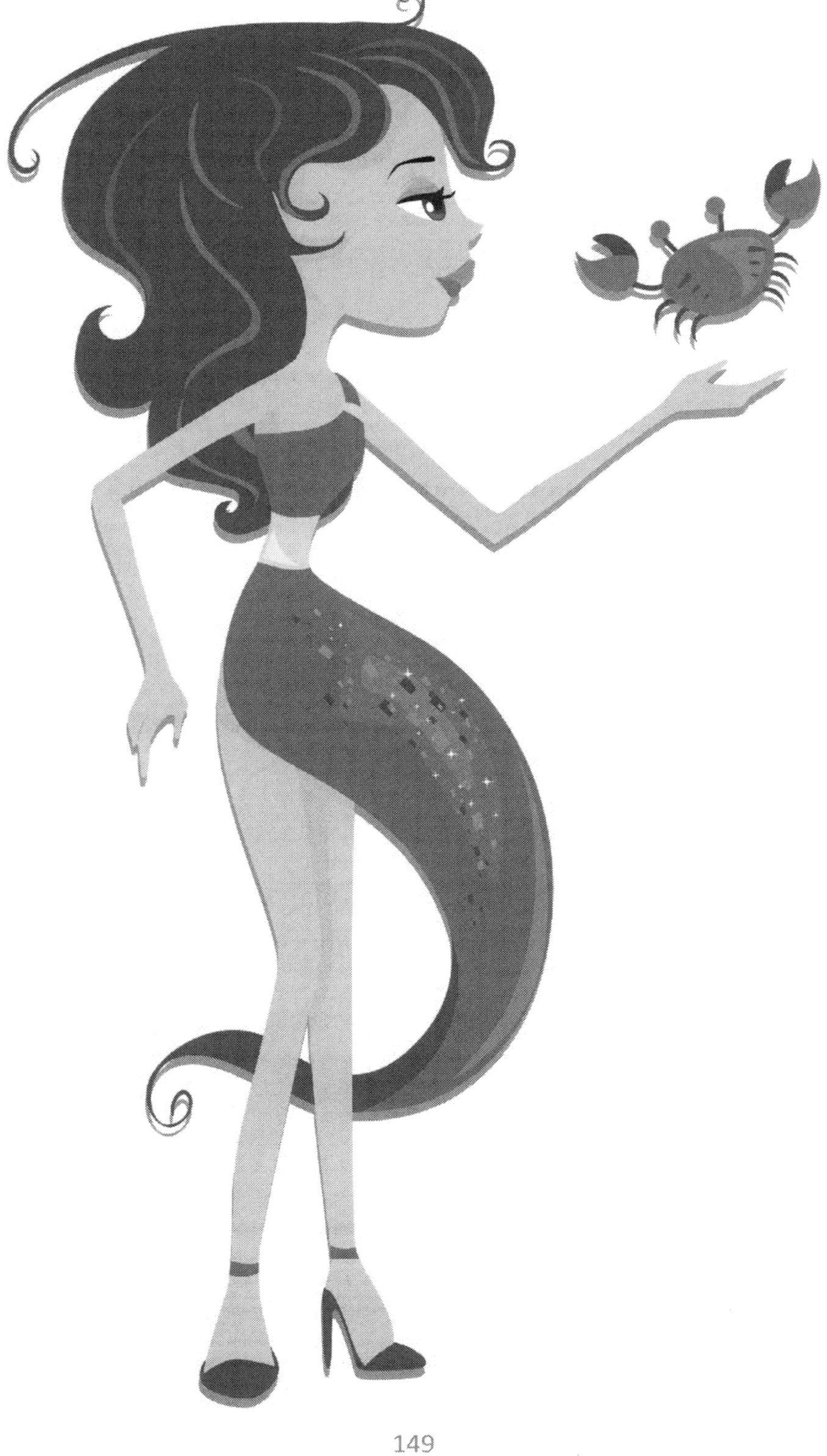

New Moon

Beaver Moon

October/November

30 Monday

You are entering a time that grows your life. A goal comes into focus; it brings abundance and magic to the forefront of your world. There is a shift ahead that brings new foundations. It improves stability, and this security lets you smash your goals. Moving forward from a grounded and balanced foundation kickstarts a cycle of growth and prosperity. New options soon arrive that support your vision for future growth.

31 Tuesday ~ Samhain/Halloween, All Hallows Eve Venus trine Uranus 12:51

Embrace a magical and vibrant Halloween under the influence of an engaging and dynamic Venus trine Uranus aspect that adds a dash of spontaneity and fun into your life. It promotes expansion as you connect with a broader circle of friends. Forging friendships and getting involved with your social life offers sound foundations with more excellent stability and balance.

1 Wednesday ~ All Saints' Day

Dynamic options arrive that encourage growth and learning. It begins an enriching phase as you plot a course towards advancing your career path. As you move towards expansion, Working with your abilities brings a highly productive chapter that enables you to set your sights on a lofty goal. It brings a significant focus on improving your bottom line, and indeed, you soon create inroads towards your vision.

2 Thursday

Developments ahead bring news and potential into your life. The correct option crops up that feels like the perfect fit for your situation. An emphasis on improving your circumstances brings a bumper crop of potential to your door. You attract possibilities that let you dip your toes into a new area of interest worth your time.

NOVEMBER

3 Friday ~ Sun opposed Jupiter 5:02. Venus opposed Neptune at 22:05

The Sun opposed Jupiter transit brings the increasing potential for wealth and good fortune. Rising prospects see things in your life fall in place as you turn a corner and head towards a lucky streak. Changes ahead connect you with a prosperous chapter. It offers benefits that shine a light on an expansive and optimistic time of growth. As you develop unique goals centered around your gifts and talents, you promote creativity and amplify possible potential.

4 Saturday ~ Taurids Meteor Shower. Sept 7th - Dec 10th
Saturn turns direct in Pisces at 7:15. Mercury opposed Uranus 16:06

The Mercury opposed Uranus transit brings a chaotic and hectic pace. The busier pace may leave you feeling tense, anxious, and scattered. Uranus adds an unexpected dash, leaving you scrambling to deal with surprise news. Information emerges out of the left field, leaving you wondering what will happen next. Focusing on the basics improves balance.

5 Sunday ~ Last Quarter Moon in Leo 08:37

You ride a wave of hopeful energy that offers a more sustained positive trend for your life. It draws heightened creativity, which helps you see tremendous gains in your world as you open your life to innovative solutions. It offers a path that triggers a robust phase of activity and happiness. Positive news ahead draws a fresh opportunity that helps you pivot towards an exciting area. It enables you to reap the rewards of expanding your life.

NOVEMBER

6 Monday ~ Venus trine Pluto 14:38

Today's Venus trine with Pluto adds intensity to your love life. This aspect turns up the heat in your personal life. Sexual attraction and passion rise as you get busy developing your personal life. Singles are likely to find new romance soon, while couples can embrace a more connected and sizzling love life. It grows a journey that provides many unique experiences for your life. You dive into an enriching landscape that promotes harmony and happiness.

7 Tuesday ~ Mercury trine Neptune 1:36

Creativity, imagination, and innovation blaze a wildfire of inspiration as Mercury and Neptune form a trine today. Increased sensitivity to this vibrational energy attracts a boost into your world that bolsters vitality. It offers a dramatic shift that helps you quickly learn or develop a new area. Creating a plan and mapping out your vision for future growth will help connect you with a journey that offers a positive result.

8 Wednesday ~ Venus ingress Libra 9:27

A new possibility crops up and brings an enterprising chapter that offers stable foundations. Your life lights up with new potential, and taking matters into your own hands draws a fruitful result. A decisive time enables you to reach for your dreams proactively. It helps you go after a high-level assignment that deepens your talents and refines your skills. It reveals an area that holds promise for your working life.

9 Thursday ~ Mercury sextile Pluto 12:16

Today, the Mercury sextile Pluto transit adds extra layers and dimensions to your creative thinking. It brings an ideal time for research, planning, and mapping out unique areas for future development. Your penetrating inquiries delve deep and help you discover any potential pitfalls and issues. Your inquiring mind places you in a solid position to grow your dreams as you do due diligence and understand all aspects of your investigations.

November

10 Friday ~ Veterans Day (Observed), Mercury ingress Sagittarius 6:22, Mercury square Saturn 15:07

Today's Mercury square Saturn challenges critical thinking skills and intrepid enquiring. Tensions could flare up and lead to disruptions. Miscommunication is more likely when you are not on the same page as the person you talk to about your thoughts and ideas. Being adaptable and patient places you in prime alignment to balance the path ahead.

11 Saturday ~ Veterans Day, Remembrance Day (Canada), Mars opposed Uranus 21:11

The Mars opposed Uranus could catch you off guard today, leading to tension in personal bonds. An unexpected tension could flare up, causing an argument or dispute with a family member or loved one. Trusting your gut instincts is illuminating. As you navigate the way ahead with grace and flexibility, you understand the blocks that limit progress.

12 Sunday

A focus on the past shines brightly when someone from your previous chapter bridges the gap. It has you feeling a warm glow of sentimentality as you traverse memories and catch up with the news with this individual. It draws an active time of sharing thoughts and ideas that enrich your life with a sense of connection. It brings friendship and fun into your world. It lets you make tracks towards improving your social life as you taste adventure with this person.

November

13 Monday ~ New Moon in Scorpio 09:27, Sun opposed Uranus 17:20

The Sun opposed Uranus transit attracts a restless vibe that gives you the green light to try something new and different. It drives a liberating chapter that offers spontaneity as you get busy expressing your unique individual melody and personality. Things fall into place with a sense of synchronicity as you move to an active and dynamic time. Experimenting and exploring various options brings the right flavor into your life. It positions you correctly to achieve growth.

14 Tuesday

News arrives that cracks the code to developing your life. You discover the right project to sink your teeth into, which inspires your life. It offers sound foundations that draw stability, security, and balance. It rekindles vitality and has you feeling motivated to take on new projects and expand your horizons. As you grow and widen the borders of your life, you discover new areas that carry you forward towards greener pastures.

15 Wednesday ~ Mercury sextile Venus 12:47

A loving vibe helps you get past hump day. Today's Mercury sextile Venus adds a positive influence that harmonizes and nurtures well-being in your world. Less stress and more enjoyment grow solid foundations. Personal relationships benefit from open communication leading to fulfillment. Communication arrives that shines the light around deepening friendships. An opportunity for collaboration offers growth and a sense of kinship.

16 Thursday

You are poised to clear out negative energy and draw balance into your foundations. It begins a chapter of awakening that illuminates a solid foundation to grow your dreams. You head towards growth, which lets you make transparent and salient progress on developing goals. Your intuition guides you towards a beautiful journey of self-development and fulfillment.

November

17 Friday ~ Leonids Meteor Shower November 6-30th, Mars trine Neptune 8:36, Sun trine Neptune 14:51

Under the influence of Neptune, creativity soars, epiphanies and lightbulb moments are the order of the day. Little goes under your radar when you spot an opportunity that feels like the right fit for your life. It is a move in the right direction, and this helps you grow something that offers rewards. It brings an enriching time that provides a potent brew of new options.

18 Saturday ~ Sun conjunct Mars 5:41

Sun conjunct Mars brings abundant energy and initiative, and your drive to try new things increases. A desire for action can cause restlessness if not channeled and released. It dispels the heavy vibes that have felt so heavy. Attractive possibilities emerge that tempt you forward. It brings sunny skies that soothe your restless spirit. It connects with a social aspect that draws on excitement and anticipation; this helps expand your social circle.

19 Sunday

Getting involved with a beloved creative pastime rewards you with a journey you can grow. It begins a trend of making time for yourself and dabbling with a creative undertaking. It brings a time of establishing foundations; stabilizing the core elements in your life does get a shift towards a more secure environment. Your potential for success moves forward in leaps and bounds.

November

20 Monday ~ First Quarter Moon in Aquarius 10:50, Sun sextile Pluto 21:26

Today's Sun sextile Pluto transit drives ambitions and sees you heading into the working week with an increased drive to succeed and conquer your goals. Feeling determined and purposeful enables you to nail your tasks quickly and finish work with energy still in the tank. Using planning helps create the framework to grow your vision for future growth. Linking with others is beneficial as they add their thoughts and ideas.

21 Tuesday

Good fortune is ready to blossom in your world. Planning and researching infuse your creativity with a proactive approach that brings drive and growth your way. It helps you lead as new options spark forward momentum. You enter an upbeat and optimistic time of developing goals that offer rising prospects in your world. A boost to your career path rekindles motivation and brings an enterprising time of developing skills.

22 Wednesday ~ Mars sextile Pluto 1:17, Sun ingress Sagittarius 13:59

Today's transit increases energy in the workplace. No job is too small as you take on the lot and work towards your vision. Information that crosses your path opens a productive avenue worth developing. A helping hand from someone in the background pulls the strings that open the gate to a brighter chapter in your life. It opens a clear path that sees optimism surge as the fires of inspiration begin burning again.

23 Thursday ~ Thanksgiving Day (USA), Sun square Saturn 9:46

Saturn is the ruler of honoring traditions and following rigid structures that form set boundaries. Today's square illuminates a happy time shared with loved ones, perfect with Saturn, who delights in honoring the past. You direct your attention towards sharing and spending time in a supportive and nurturing environment. A positive influence ahead lets you touch down in a vibrant landscape of possibility. It brings harmony into your life as you get involved in sharing engaging conversations and thoughtful dialogues with kindred spirits.

November

24 Friday ~ Mars ingress Sagittarius 10:10

This transit emits a rebellious vibe that rejuvenates your energy and has you seeking expansion. It lets you embrace a more connected chapter as you move away from limitations and head toward growth. An active time of mingling brings a unique friendship to light. It offers a joyful time that ignites inspiration and happiness. A focus on social engagement opens a path of sharing thoughts and ideas with a caring individual. It does bring rising prospects into your life.

25 Saturday ~ Mars square Saturn 16:57

Today's aspect can feel challenging as your mind is on Saturn's to-do list. You may find it difficult to relax and unwind when your thoughts turn to the irons you have burning in the fire. It positions you to progress towards expansion as you push back the barriers that limit progress. You are no stranger to challenge; you can soon enjoy the rewards of perseverance. Your potential range expands and lights up pathways of inspiration and excitement.

26 Sunday

A shift ahead transitions you towards a positive chapter that brings sunny skies overhead. It opens the doors to a busy time that sees you sharing with friends and family. It brings a positive social aspect that draws well-being and harmony. It places you in a solid position to get involved with a more social path. It strongly correlates to improved security and stability on the home front. A social chapter ahead washes away the stress and outworn energy.

NOVEMBER

27 Monday ~ Beaver Full Moon in Gemini 09:16, Mercury square Neptune 13:26

Today, the Mercury square Neptune aspect can distort or make mountains of molehills. It adds a dash of illusion into your business dealings that can have your head spinning with tall tales and trying to sort the truth from the exaggeration. It brings a time of restructuring that helps you balance a sensitive area. It connects you with the right conditions to progress towards a brighter chapter.

28 Tuesday

The essential news ahead brings an opportunity. It gives you an excellent chance to progress your talents. Refining your abilities brings learning and achievement to the forefront of your life. Your career path gets a boost that lets you advance faster towards your goals. It is ideal for learning a new area and embracing a chapter of rising prospects. It brings side journeys; finding the proper assignment brings dynamic progression.

29 Wednesday

You are moving in a positive direction. New possibilities are coming that tempt you towards a time of expansion. It provides you with better conditions in which to grow your life. It offers a prosperous time for social growth and draws a boost, bringing refreshing and uplifting energy. It brings a sense of purpose that enables you to investigate leads and look to side pathways that offer growth and rising prospects.

30 Thursday

You may be questioning the path ahead but feeling restless is the invitation to broaden the scope of your world by exploring new horizons. It is a catalyst for growth as it lets you move forward to a fresh start that opens new options to tempt you along. You enter a productive time that elevates prospects. It hits a high note in your social life as you expand your circle of friends. It positions you correctly to achieve growth and progress to an abundant chapter.

December

Sun	Mon	Tue	Wed	Thu	Fri	Sat
					1	2
3	4	5	6	7	8	9
10	11	12	13	14	15	16
17	18	19	20	21	22	23
24	25	26	27	28	29	30
31						

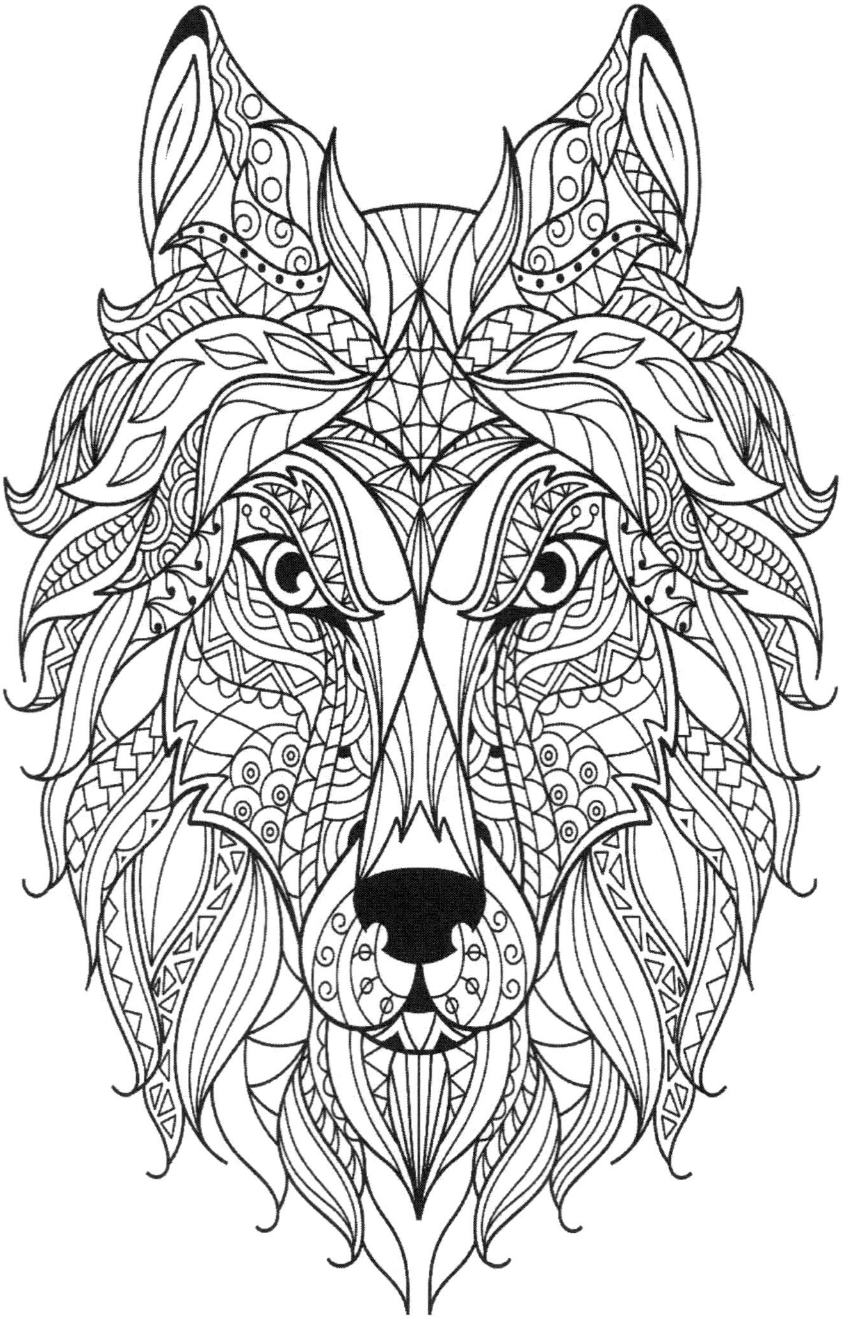

New Moon

Cold Moon

December

1 Friday ~ Mercury ingress Capricorn 14:29

Joy and harmony will flow into your world soon. It brings options that fuel desires, bringing new possibilities to light. Lighter energy hums along in the background of your life, bringing stable foundations that secure a comfortable chapter ahead. News arrives that draws a sentimental theme surrounding your world, which makes you aware of the passage of time and brings a desire to catch up with old friends.

2 Saturday ~ Mercury sextile Saturn 15:25

Today's Mercury sextile Saturn transit is favorable for organizing and streamlining your workload to create a stimulating and productive environment. Expressing authority and leadership skills create a purposeful and productive environment. It anchors you in a grounded environment that draws balance and restores equilibrium. It is a positive influence that offers grace and blessings.

3 Sunday ~ Venus square Pluto 13:29

Today's aspect could see a flare-up of jealousy or possessiveness. Your romantic partner may feel threatened by heightened social activities and invitations in the pre-run up to Christmas. Take time to support and boost confidence to help offset the Venus square Pluto aspect. Being aware of these fears' dynamics helps keep relationships healthy and balanced. Screening out distractions brings depth, purpose, structure, and balance to your life.

DECEMBER

4 Monday ~ Mercury at Greatest Elongation 21.3 E, Venus ingress Scorpio 18:48

You hear fantastic news ahead that offers a golden opportunity. It gets you back on track as prospects begin to rise. It lights a path that releases the heaviness as you get involved with a lighter journey moving forward. A new role is on offer, bringing surging optimism and a creative spark that directs your energy towards developing a venture that offers room for advancement. It brings a possibility to build a foundation that grows your abilities and refines your talents.

5 Tuesday ~ Last Quarter Moon in Virgo 05:50, Venus trine Saturn 22:51

Today's Venus trine Saturn transit is ideal for developing relationships. Self-expression, warmth, and affection flow freely under this favorable aspect. It brings an expressive chapter that offers impulsivity, experience, and connection. There is a surprise nestled ahead that leads to celebration. It brings events on the horizon that offer a chance to expand your circle of friends. It shines a light on building stable emotional foundations.

6 Wednesday ~ Neptune turns direct in Pisces, 12:38

With Neptune turning direct in Pisces, an extra emotional element adds flavor to your dreams, creativity, and vision. Wistful thinking, goals, and fantasies let you move beyond the material world and escape into fanciful thoughts about future possibilities. Alchemy is brewing in the background of your life. It heightens potential and brings unique options flowing into your world. You enter a prosperous time that offers room to grow a dream.

7 Thursday ~ Hanukkah (begins at sunset)

Stirring the pot of manifestation brings impressive results to your door. Being available to change brings a time of growth and prosperity that restores equilibrium and gives a more stable basis to the foundations in your life. Your willingness to be open to developing your world creates remarkable progress. New ideas and options arrive to tempt you forward.

December

8 Friday ~ Mercury trine Jupiter 4:04

Mercury's trine Jupiter transit today ignites the possibility of heightened intuition and attracts a chance to chill with friends. It connects you with a social environment that stabilizes foundations and draws abundance into your life. It puts dreams front and center and offers a bumper crop of potential for your social life. Sharing thoughts and ideas with like-minded people nurture well-being.

9 Saturday

Today lets you take a vital step forward towards developing your romantic life. It opens the door to a unique chapter that nurtures your life. You reawaken to the rich landscape of potential surrounding your love life. Deepening the bond with someone who offers thoughtful conversations draws harmony and happiness into your life. It brings the ideal conditions to advance your personal life forward. Opportunities are sweeping in, leaving you feeling refreshed.

10 Sunday ~ Venus opposed Jupiter 3:34

This astrological transit adds an indulgent vibration and has you wanting to explore hedonism, romance, and magic. The pursuit of pleasure attracts social engagement, relaxation, and unwinding with a leisurely influence restoring well-being. It brings a journey of growing your world and sharing experiences and thoughts with a broader range of friends. Lively conversations and draw renewal and rejuvenation.

December

11 Monday ~ Mercury sextile Venus 19:22

Communication flows freely into your social life, attracting invitations and mingling opportunities. The Mercury sextile Venus aspect nurtures stable foundations. News arrives soon that offers information that bodes well for developing a new area in your life. It provides a highly productive cycle as you connect with a broader circle of friends. Forging friendships and getting involved with your social life offers sound foundations.

12 Tuesday ~ New Moon in Sagittarius 23:32

Opportunities ahead bring a positive aspect that cleans the slate. It prepares you for a new cycle of potential that enables you to turn a corner as it gets an active growth process and possibility ahead. It jumpstarts a journey that progresses life forward towards developing your social life. It lets you kick the cobwebs to the curb and enjoy a flood of invitations to mingle and network with your broader circle of friends.

13 Wednesday ~ Mercury turns Retrograde in Capricorn 7:08
Geminids Meteor Shower Dec 7-17th

Mercury turns retrograde, seeing some communication issues cropping up over the next few weeks. Plans and times quickly become mixed as messages scramble during this more chaotic planetary phase. Taking time to restore balance and offering clear communication to others can help minimize mixed messages during the retrograde phase.

14 Thursday

Good fortune enters your life when you hear excellent news soon. It draws a surprise that offers change and progression. It brings a chance to catch up with friends you haven't seen for a while—mingling with your social circle lights a delightful path of friendship and fun. It draws rejuvenation and joy into your social life. It ushers in active, lively discussions that offer new ideas and options.

December

15 Friday ~ Hanukkah (ends at sunset)

You receive enchanting information which promotes harmony and happiness. It lights a path forward for your social life, and you soon get busy with invitations out and about. Good fortune arrives with a flurry of excitement, which brings opportunities to mingle. Spending time with companions draws a relaxed environment that nourishes your spirit. You discover you can grow your life in many ways as the borders of your world expand outwardly.

16 Saturday

A friend from your broader social circle has been mulling over the bond with you and thinking about getting in touch. They hope to share news and thoughts that deepen the bond. They feel that sharing supportive conversations will reveal a path that offers room to progress forward. It brings a new beginning that provides a chance to develop a journey with an attentive and engaging person.

17 Sunday

A new and vital chapter is coming. It brings a beautiful sense of happiness as you reboot the potential in your world. It brings activity afoot that offers a social aspect. It is a breath of fresh air that brings new possibilities to light. The way forward is bright and optimistic; new options arrive to tempt you towards growth and artistic expression. It gives you a chance to rebrand your image and reinvent yourself in a new area. It drives a phase of wanderlust and adventure.

DECEMBER

18 Monday ~ Mercury trine Jupiter 14:33

Mercury trine Jupiter transit brings optimism, luck, and good news. Information arrives that bodes well for your social life. Indeed, it's easy to make new friends under this favorable influence that sparks social engagement and thoughtful discussions with friendly characters. It brings good fortune that opens an exciting avenue forward. Something special comes into your world that sets the stage for an active and dynamic chapter ahead.

19 Tuesday ~ First Quarter Moon in Pisces 18:39

You reveal an opportunity that broadens your horizons. Nurturing this environment brings happiness and success. It lights a path forward towards developing a dream. Casting your net of possibilities comprehensive enables you to be open and willing to explore new options. It encourages the type of expansion that supports well-being and self-development. It launches a direction that offers room to grow your talents.

20 Wednesday

A new venture emerges that offers the exciting prospect of success. It sends shimmering rays of creativity that provide fertile ground to generate ideas. It brings change and a new direction that sets you on a path of progress. It opens your life up to new areas and teaches you techniques that refine your abilities. It brings the right platform in which to express your artistic expression. It draws a fateful time of positive influences that brings new options to your table.

21 Thursday ~ Ursids Meteor Shower Dec 17th – 25th, Venus opposed Uranus 7:04, Mercury sextile Saturn 12:35

Today's Venus opposed Uranus alignment brings growth to personal relationships. Increasing synergy and chemistry could spark a new romance or flirtation opportunity. Things are on the move in your life. It helps you sweep away what no longer serves your highest good. It brings an environment that heightens confidence as you lift the lid on a journey that beckons you forward.

December

22 Friday ~ Sun ingress Capricorn 3:24, Yule/Winter Solstice 03:28, Sun conjunct Mercury 18:53

The Sun conjunct Mercury aspect favors communication. It brings the sharing of thoughtful dialogues and entertaining discussions. Life ahead lines up to support your efforts to improve the foundations of your life. It brings the gift of security and abundance. It draws social opportunities and lively discussions that reveal an uplifting time shared with friends.

23 Saturday ~ Mercury ingress Sagittarius 6:19

You spend time in a supportive and nurturing environment. Events align to nourish your soul and expand the borders of your world. It illustrates a time of lively discussions that offer an open road of potential in your life. There will be a chance to plan a trip away, something to work on to bring a goal into focus. The road forward suddenly clears when an offer arrives. It stirs the pot of manifestation, bringing impressive results to your door.

24 Sunday ~ Sun sextile Saturn 17:28

Sun sextile Saturn transit lends patience to family gatherings, which can be a godsend if your family dynamics tend to be challenging. An emphasis on building stable foundations draws peace and grounded energy. It paves the way for better communication that clears the air. Nurturing family ties offers a lighter energy flow that restores well-being and connects you with meaningful areas.

DECEMBER

25 Monday ~ Christmas Day, Venus trine Neptune 17:15

Venus trine Neptune transit is the perfect backdrop to Christmas. It attracts creativity, well-being, and fulfillment. This transit favors singing, music, and delight in the day's celebration. Support flows into your world, which offers room to improve your social life. It lets you pack in plenty of fun adventures with kindred spirits.

26 Tuesday ~ Kwanzaa begins

Life picks up the pace as a whirlwind of activity tempts you. A cluster of social opportunities helps create a hotspot of potential in your life. It underscores an atmosphere of relaxation and lively discussions. It takes you towards freedom and expansion, which generates a fresh start of new possibilities for your life. It supplies optimism, positivity, and favorable outcomes.

27 Wednesday ~ Cold Full Moon, Moon before Yule in Cancer 0:34, Mercury square Neptune 7:36, Sun trine Jupiter 15:28

The Sun trine Jupiter aspect lights up good fortune across the board. New possibilities blossom as a favorable wind ignites your passion and imagination. It is an excellent time to plan and reflect on future goals. You have a lot you hope to accomplish; planning and preparation enable you to head towards growth.

28 Thursday ~ Mercury conjunct Mars 0:26, Mars square Neptune 22:15

The Mars square Neptune aspect brings surprising news that links you with developing a journey that aligns with the person you are becoming. You improve circumstances through a willingness to broaden your horizons. Developing your skills and growing your talents link you with positive change. Life brings opportunities that offer a new source of prosperity in your world. Refining this potential connects with learning and creativity.

December

29 Friday ~ Venus sextile Pluto 6:00, Venus ingress Sagittarius 20:21

The Venus sextile Pluto transit deepens romantic love and grows relationship potential. It brings an expressive time of nurturing a wellspring of abundance in your world. Life becomes a whirlwind most positively. It carries news, and this is a boost to your mood. As you lift the lid on a fresh chapter, the fires of your inspiration burn brightly. Nurturing your dreams gets you in touch with a path you can embrace growing.

30 Saturday

A river of lightness brings a rare aspect that draws new possibilities to light. You discover a gemstone of an option that is rocket fuel for your creativity. It helps you take steps towards realizing a long-held dream. It brings an artistic project that debuts your talents to a broader audience. It connects you with kindred spirits who offer engaging discussions and advice.

31 Sunday ~ New Year's Eve, Jupiter turns direct in Taurus at 2:41

In a promising sign, Jupiter turns direct on New Year's Eve. It foretells bright blessings, good fortune, and opportunities on the horizon. Unlimited possibilities spark inspiration and wonder. It brings an optimistic chapter with room to flex your social muscle with friends. Spending time in a community environment draws vital energy that nourishes your well-being. It opens the door to a journey that draws enriching experiences.

Astrology & Horoscope Books.

https://mystic-cat.com/

Printed in Great Britain
by Amazon